Blenheim
Britain's Fastest World War Two Bomber

KEY
Books

HISTORIC MILITARY AIRCRAFT SERIES, VOL 31

Published by Key Books
An imprint of Key Publishing Ltd
PO Box 100
Stamford
Lincs PE9 1XQ

www.keypublishing.com

Original editions published as *Aeroplane Icons: Blenheim* © 2011, edited by Martyn Chorlton

This edition © 2023

ISBN 978 1 80282 705 7

Typeset by Focused on Design Ltd, UK.

Contents

Bristol Type 142, K7557, the foundation block of the Blenheim story. (*Aeroplane*)

Introduction

To say the Blenheim caused a stir when it was introduced to RAF squadrons in early 1937 is a bit of an understatement. Its superb performance made it the RAF's fastest bomber for many years and, before the arrival of the Hurricane and Spitfire, also the fast aircraft in the entire inventory. Under the pre-war Expansion Schemes, the Blenheim single-handedly dragged the RAF out of the doldrums into a new modern age.

The Blenheim achieved a whole host of 'firsts', despite never originating as a military requirement. The bomber was the RAF's first all-metal monoplane with a semi-monocoque, stressed-skinned construction and the first to have hydraulically-operated retractable undercarriage, flaps and power-turret, not to mention the variable-pitch propellers. The way it was built was also ground-breaking, seeing the introduction of sectionalised production. This involved the aircraft being broken down into substantial sections, each of which was built, complete with all equipment and necessary sub-assemblies which were all incorporated into a fluid production line. It set the standard for how virtually all British aircraft were constructed from 1936 onwards, the Avro Lancaster as an example, benefited enormously from applying this technique.

By the beginning of the Second World War, over 1,000 were on RAF charge, even though by then the type was clearly obsolete compared to its German counterparts. Regardless, we need to consider where we would have been without it. The Fairey Battle would have been on its own in France and this would inevitably have resulted in even worse losses than they already suffered, which is hard to imagine.

The Blenheim would also suffer heavy losses but this was through no fault of the aircraft or the brave crews who constantly faced overwhelming odds. The aircraft was being operated in an environment where it stood little chance; i.e. at low-level and in daylight. The Blenheim was totally let down by tactics which may have worked well during pre-war exercises, but certainly did not work in the heat of battle. Despite the heavy losses it suffered, the type continued to be used in North Africa in the same way and for this it would once again pay the price.

Fortunately to help us remember the efforts of all the brave aircrew that were felled flying the Blenheim, several examples have been preserved across the world.

Chapter 1

Barnwell's Brainchild

The story of the Blenheim has its roots firmly embedded within a civilian project first envisaged by Frank Barnwell and his design team at the Bristol Aeroplane Company, Filton, in early 1933. The plan was to produce a commercial light transport aircraft capable of cruising at a minimum speed of 250mph.

By late July 1933, Barnwell, closely supported by Leslie Frise, had transcribed his ideas for the new aircraft onto paper. This revealed a twin-engined, low-wing monoplane with a monocoque enclosed cockpit and a fuselage capable of holding two crew and six passengers in comfort. Power was planned to be a pair of Bristol Aquila I sleeve-valve, air cooled radial engines producing 500hp each. However, the Aquila was still under development with a team of Bristol engineers led by A H R 'Roy' Fedden and was not destined to be ready until September 1934.

Without any authority for construction of a prototype, Barnwell allocated the Bristol designation Type 135 to his new light twin which was sending waves of enthusiasm throughout the company. It was both a pleasant and fortuitous coincidence that the owner of the *Daily Mail*, Lord Rothermere, a strong supporter of British aviation, was on a personal campaign to own 'the fastest commercial aeroplane in Europe'. This ambition was mainly driven by advances in civilian aviation across the Atlantic, with the USA making very strong claims (not unjustifiable) of the potential of their new Douglas DC-1. Local

The Bristol Type 142, being put through its paces by Bristol's Chief Test Pilot Cyril Uwins in 1935. (*Aeroplane*)

The Type 142 taxies to the grass runway at Filton with Cyril Uwins at the controls. (*Aeroplane*)

reporter R T Lewis, who worked for the *Bristol Evening News*, was being kept fully informed of the progress of the Type 135 and, without delay, passed on what he knew to Lord Rothermere. The media baron gave Lewis just one week to find out all of the details of the design.

On March 6, 1934, Barnwell gave Lewis an estimated performance of 240mph at 6,500ft for the Type 135, if fitted with part-supercharged Bristol Mercury engines in lieu of the Aquilas. Lewis, without delay, passed the information on to Lord Rothermere. On March 26, Lewis phoned Roy Fedden to pass on Rothermere's desire to have a single Type 135 built for his private use.

Rather than greeting this firm order with enthusiasm, the directors at Bristol treated the order with 'mild apprehension'. The reason for this was that Lord Rothermere had a reputation as a 'campaigner' in both the journalistic and political worlds while the senior staff at Bristol were walking a more diplomatic line. Rothermere's reasons for purchasing the Type 135 were admirable. His first intention was to use the aircraft to promote civilian aviation across Britain, in particular the advantages that it could bring to business. His second intention was more 'maverick', as he wanted the aircraft to provide him with sufficient 'ammunition' to expend at the Air Ministry by owning a civilian aircraft that could easily outpace the fastest RAF fighters of the day. This was where Bristol was particularly uncomfortable, because for many years the Air Ministry had been by far its best customer and it did not want to upset this working relationship.

To clear the air, the senior staff of the company organised a meeting in London on March 29 with Lord Rothermere, who was still very keen to get his hands on the aircraft. Furthermore, he offered to pay £18,500 for the Type 135's construction, half once the contract was signed and the remainder in a year's time if the aircraft was in the air by then.

Still playing a cautious game, the directors then approached the Air Ministry, delicately presenting them with an outline of Lord Rothermere's proposals. They need not have worried, because the Air Ministry was as enthusiastic as Lord Rothermere about the Type 135. Without any further delay, the project began to gain momentum. Barnwell was encouraged by the Air Ministry's response and the idea of the aircraft being used for military purposes was never far from his mind.

The Type 142 and 143

The general air of encouragement permeating throughout Filton in early 1934 resulted in

The generous trailing edge split-flaps of the Type 142 that run the entire length of wing, only ending where they meet the ailerons. The flaps were all made of Alclad sheet with flanged ribs. (*Aeroplane*)

Barnwell also proposing an Aquila-powered version of the Type 135 which would use up to 70% of the original design's components. Redesigned with Mercury engines, the Type 135 was redesignated as the Type 142 while the Aquila-powered aircraft, which was to be built at the same time, was known as the Type 143. Apart from its power plant, the latter only differed by having a sharper nose profile and a larger fuselage which could cater for eight passengers and two crew.

The undercarriage of the Type 142 hydraulically retracted backwards, independently into the engine nacelles. The Dunlop-tyred wheels were mounted between two oleo-pneumatic struts which absorb the landing shocks, one of many unique, ground-breaking features of the aircraft. (*Aeroplane*)

The pleasing lines of Type 142 K7557 are evident in this photo, taken at Filton in Autumn 1935. Crew and passenger comfort were not lacking and visibility for both was also good. The passengers not only enjoyed large windows in the side of the cabin but also three 'skylights' along the spine. (*Aeroplane*)

It was not long before the Type 143 generated some foreign interest from Finland, who were keen on a militarised version of the aircraft. The Finn's attention was later drawn away from the Type 143 when the Type 142 burst onto the scene in early 1935. On April 12, 1935 in the hands of Cyril Uwins, the Type 142 made its first, uneventful flight from Filton. Despite being registered as G-ADCZ on February 25, these letters were never carried and, during Lord Rothermere's brief ownership of the aircraft, it was privately named *Britain First*.

Not long after the aircraft's first flight, the Air Ministry's ongoing interest in the project manifested itself still further in a letter received from the Chief of Air Staff stating: '…I agree… that the Bristol twin should be considered as a medium bomber if the Bristol Aircraft Company have a reasonable proposition to put forward for the supply of this type in reasonable numbers. In this connection I suggest that we should offer to test the aircraft made for Lord Rothermere at Martlesham free of charge in order to ascertain its performance and characteristics.'

The Type 143 G-ADEK running up its Aquila engines at Filton in 1936. Note the 'groundcrew' with a small extinguisher in his pocket and a sign behind, of the rapid expansion of Filton's facilities. (*Aeroplane*)

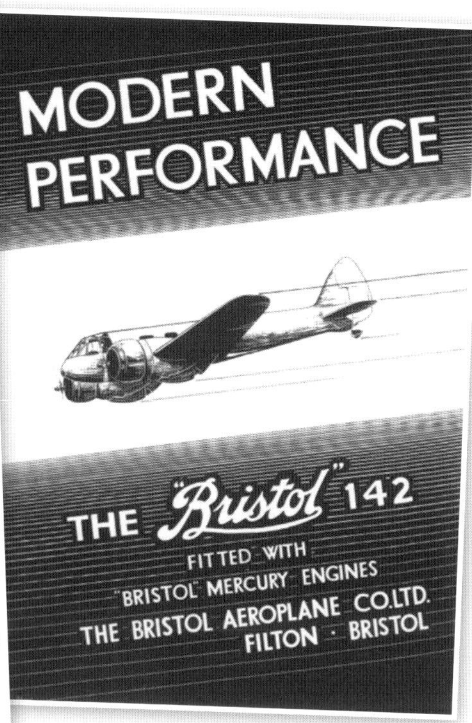

Below: Photographs of the Type 142 displaying anything other than its military serial K7557 are rare. The aircraft is seen here with the experimental registration R-12 before being delivered to the A&AEE at Martlesham Heath in June 1935 for trials. (via Martyn Chorlton)

After Lord Rothermere was approached, he willingly donated the Type 142 to the Air Council and, by June 1935, the aircraft was wearing the experimental serial 'R-12' on its fuselage after arriving with the A&AEE at Martlesham Heath. Services trials revealed some very impressive performance figures, including 285mph with a maximum load and a maximum speed of 307mph. These figures indicated that the Type 142 was between 15% and 20% faster than the quickest front line RAF fighter.

After being returned to Bristol in July 1935, the company proposed a bomber variant of the aircraft, designated the Type 142M. Such interest being generated in the Type 142 completely overshadowed the work that had already been done on the Type 143. The Aquila engines were not ready until late 1935 and, on January 20, 1936, wearing the registration R-14, the Type 143 first flew from Filton, once again with Cyril Uwins at the controls. The aircraft was destined never to leave its Bristol home and continued flying as G-ADEK until 1938 as a test-bed for the Aquila until the engine was abandoned. By 1940, the Type 143 was unceremoniously scrapped at Filton.

The Type 142, now sporting the military serial K7557, continued to incorporate Bristol modifications and went on to fly further trials with RAE in April 1936. After briefly giving 24 and 101 Squadrons a taste of things to come, K7557 returned to the A&AEE in late 1936 and then, by April 1937, it was back with the RAE. Grounded by 1940, this pioneering aircraft saw out its days at 10 SoTT at Kirkham before being scrapped in 1944.

The Type 142 presents us with a nice viewpoint of the massive drag-producing 'apron' type wheel fairings which retracted neatly over the undercarriage, leaving only a small section of the tyre exposed. The original four-blade wooden propellers were replaced by the much neater and far more efficient American-produced Hamilton-Standard variable-pitch three-blade propeller pictured here. (*Aeroplane*)

Chapter 2

The Royal Air Force's New 'Medium' Bomber

It was July 1935 when Frank Barnwell put forward his proposal for a bomber version of the Type 142. Designated the Type 142M, and later referred to as the Blenheim Mk I, the design differed in many crucial ways from the Type 142, ways which were necessary to turn the aircraft into a useful military machine. All of these features are covered in the period *Aeroplane* article which follows and it is interesting to hear them described only three months after the aircraft entered RAF service.

The Bristol Blenheim

From The Aeroplane, *June 16, 1937 (not credited)*

BLENHEIM WAS, FOR MARLBOROUGH, one of a long line of famous successes. Now, two centuries later, it is the same for Bristols. Once again Blenheim follows the effort to make 'Britain First'.

Details of the three-seat Bristol Blenheim high-speed medium-bomber (two 840 h.p. Mercury VIIIs) have now been released. Figures which can be published give the speed with full load at 15,000 ft. as 279 m.p.h. But this figure is well below the absolute maximum speed which is somewhere above 300 m.p.h. The Blenheim takes 8.8 minutes to climb to 15,000 ft –again with full load. So that works out at a climb of 1,360 ft. per min. The service ceiling is given as 30,000 ft. (9,150 m.), the take-off run as 840 yds., and the landing run as 400 yds.

The Bristol Aeroplane Co. were pioneers of all-metal stressed skin construction for aeroplanes. In the 1934 Paris Aero Show they exhibited the fuselage of the aeroplane which later became famous as Lord Rothermere's *Britain First*. This machine had such a surprisingly good performance that the Air Ministry used it as a prototype for a new range of medium-bombers. And from it evolved the Blenheim, the fastest machine of its type in the World.

(Aeroplane)

The sleek and slippery Type 142M fresh out of the factory, bearing no identifying marks, in June 1936. (*Aeroplane*)

Parked on a quiet side of Filton, the first Type 142M, now registered as K7033, is photographed in early July 1936 before departing for Martlesham Heath for its service trials. Note, the spinners were a short-lived feature as no significant aerodynamic advantage was gained from their use. (*Aeroplane*)

The highly-polished all-metal skin of K7033 gleams under the artificial light at the Paris Salon de Aéronautique on November 19, 1936. (*Aeroplane*)

Though the original design was not intended for military purposes, the Blenheim has turned out to be outstandingly successful. What Bristols can and will do when they design a comparable type from the start will be interesting.

The most noticeable difference between the Blenheim Type 142M and the *'Britain First'* Type 142 is that the new machine is a mid-wing instead of a low-wing monoplane. The reason for this is the need for the stowage of the military load rather than from aerodynamic considerations. But the change has in fact put several extra m.p.h. onto the top speed. Recently, we had an opportunity to see the imposing assembly-line of Blenheims in the Bristol works at Filton.

Incidentally, the vast new assembly-shop is one of the lightest and most airy we have ever come across. Inside, working conditions must be almost ideal. Mr. Proctor Gregg of the Bristol company was extraordinarily helpful in smoothing our path and we learned some interesting points from Mr. George White, son of Sir Stanley White, Bart., the Managing Director. Quite a number of Blenheims have been dispatched to the Service and more leave the factory each week. Each is clad in its sombre coat of many colours, though all of them Puritanical and severe on the most pleasing curves.

Aerodynamically the Bristol Blenheim is a two-motor mid-wing cantilever monoplane with all modern conveniences, or inconveniences, retractable undercart, split trailing-edge flaps, c.p. airscrews, and controllable-gilled cowling. Structurally, the Blenheim is all metal with a stressed skin.

An interesting point is that the machine is jig-built in six main sections, each of which can be easily taken from place to place, each being entirely independent of the other. The fuselage is built up in three sections.

The rear fuselage is a completely monocoque affair and extends from the tail unit to the centre section. Inverted two-section hoops are spaced at approximately 12-in. intervals. Slots are cut round

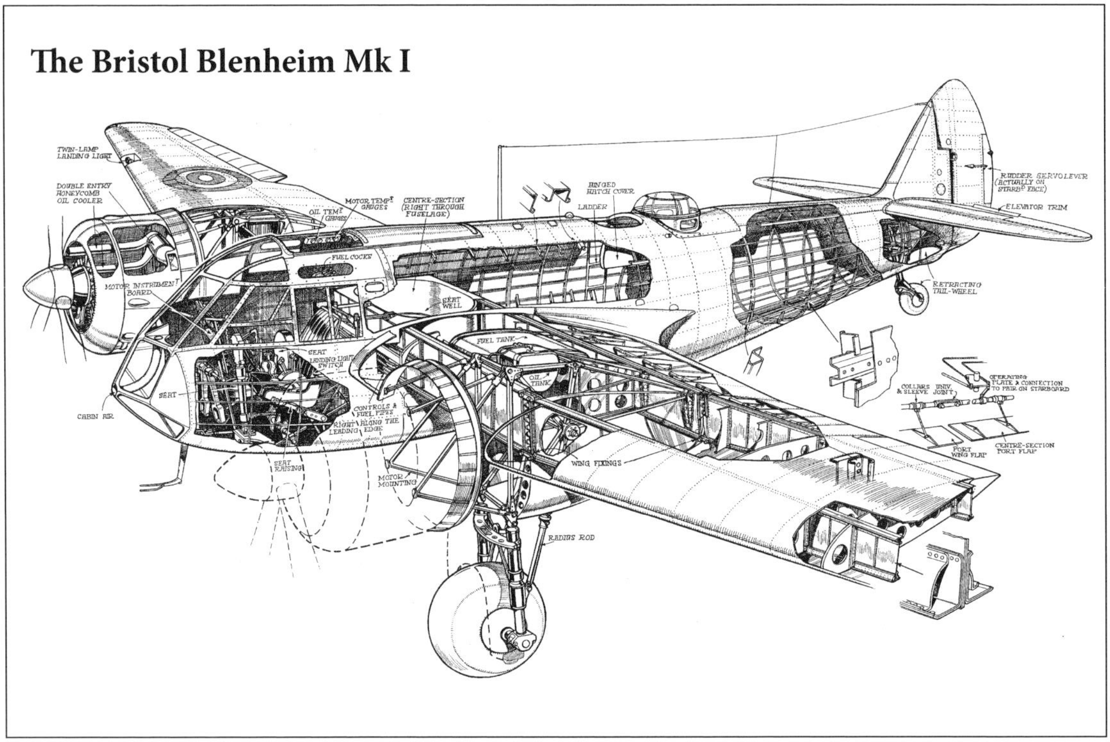

The Bristol Blenheim Mk I

The imposing assembly-line of Blenheims in the Bristol works at Filton.

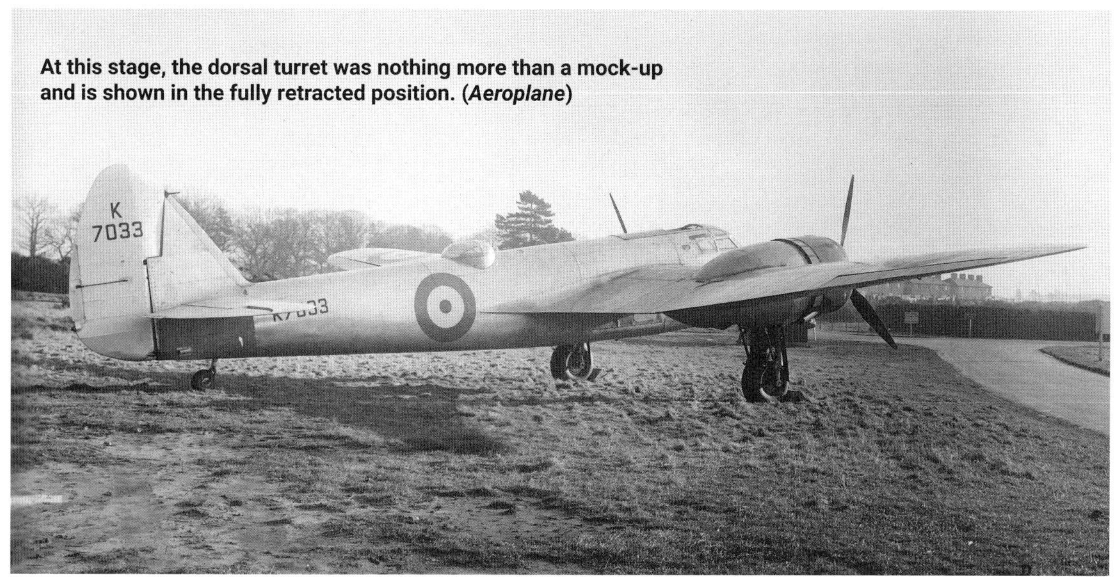

At this stage, the dorsal turret was nothing more than a mock-up and is shown in the fully retracted position. (*Aeroplane*)

the circumference at about 6-in. intervals to pass the longitudinal stringers. They are of inverted bowler-hat section. The metal skin is riveted to their crowns. The metal plating is laid in longitudinal planks overlapped downwards and backwards and riveted to the stringers and to the flanges of the hoops.

The centre-section of the wings is bolted and riveted onto the rear section of the fuselage.

The centre-section is built up on two main spars. These pass through the centre of the cabin and they leave about 40 ins between the top of each spar and the roof of the cabin.

The spars are bolted and riveted to the lower part of the fuselage. The spars are built-up with two heavy high-tensile steel flanges and a light single-plate Alclad web between them. This is strengthened by vertical bowler-hat section stringers riveted through their brims. The ribs are made from Alclad sheets with flanged edges and lipped lightening holes. The Alclad covering is riveted to the flanges of the spars and of the ribs. In the space between the spars in the fuselage, a well is cut out.

Immediately outboard of the fuselage and in the centre-section of the wings are the fuel tanks. There is one 140 gallon tank on each side, secured with the usual type of straps. The tanks can be easily removed through the lower surface of the wing. Bolted onto the spar outboard of the tanks is the square steel-tube structure which forms the frame for the undercart and the attachment for the motor-mounting.

The undercart is hydraulically retracted backwards into the motor nacelles. Each leg is entirely independent, each Dunlop-tyred wheel is mounted between two oleo-pneumatic struts which absorb the landing shocks.

Retraction is by a Bristol hydraulic-jack which breaks the knee-jointed radius rods. In the retracted position, the tyre remains below the nacelle. This is an obvious point for future refinement. Because of the middle wing, the projecting tyres could serve no useful purpose in a wheels-up landing. If there was a bomb load in the centre section of the fuselage which would bear the brunt of such a landing, the machine might disperse itself in pieces faster than even it attained as a composite whole.

The wings are built up on the same two-spar principle as the centre-section to which they are bolted through the flanges and the webs. The wing-tips are attached separately. A double landing-lamp is fitted in a transparent panel in the leading edge of the port wing.

The split trailing-edge flaps run from the side of the fuselage to the ailerons. The flaps are in two sections on each side. They are made of Alclad sheet with flanged ribs.

The flaps are operated by a long tube which runs along the trailing edge of the wing. It is moved laterally by a bell-crank lever and operates a linkage to raise and lower the flaps.

The ailerons are metal framed with a spruce leading edge and are fabric covered. They are balanced both aerodynamically and statically. Small trimming-tabs on each aileron can be adjusted from the ground.

The front portion of the fuselage is assembled separately from the rest of the machine. The bottom part is a continuation of the monocoque construction but the upper part is tubular and panelled in Perspex. The pilot sits on the left-hand side. Dual control is only fitted to a few machines and the instruments are not duplicated.

View forwards and downwards is excellent. Though the very large motor cowlings on each side of the cabin are so closely set, they do not act as blinkers as much as photographs seem to indicate. The view backwards and sideways is quite fair through the transparent panel over the cockpit. This panel slides back to form an emergency exit.

The single fin and tail-plane are attached to the stem frame which forms the extreme rear end of the fuselage. It also houses the retractable tail-wheel which folds up backwards into a boxed hole at the same time as the main undercart. The tail-wheel is fully swivelling and is carried in a fork below the shock-absorber unit.

The Type 149 was originally named the Bolingbroke, a name which was later taken up by the Canadians for their version of the Blenheim. This is a wooden mock-up of the prototype Mk IV, K7072 showing the redesigned nose compartment.

"BRITISH AND BEST. – The latest version of the Bristol Blenheim which, with two 920hp Bristol Mercury VII aero-motors and two Rotol constant-speed airscrews, is the best looking bomber at the Paris Aero Show. We have been told by those who know that there are more Bristol Blenheims flying in the World today than any other type of bomber." (*Aeroplane* November 30, 1938)

The fixed tail-plane has two spars, Alclad former-ribs and is covered with Alclad sheet. The fin is made in the same way. The sternpost bears the rudder hinges. Both rudder and elevators are built up with a metal frame and fabric-covered.

The rudder is operated through a Servo tab. The elevators have normal trimming tabs.

Controls to the motors, the ailerons and the flaps run along the leading edge of the wings and thence back through the wings where necessary. The turns are negotiated through bell-crank levers. The tail-control cables run along the bottom of the fuselage.

The two Bristol Mercury VIII motors are mounted on the centre-line of the wings. They are enclosed in long-chord cowlings with controllable gills for cooling. Each drives a D.H. controllable-pitch airscrew. Presumably, these will be replaced by the Rolls-Royce-Bristol Rotol airscrews when they are ready.

The real K7072 displaying the first version of the Mk IV nose which retained the profile of the original Mk I by simply extending the cockpit area forward. (via Martyn Chorlton)

A ten-gallon tank to hold 84 gallons of oil is mounted immediately behind and above the motors. The honeycomb oil-cooler is under the cowling in front of the oil tank and has air conveyed to it by two ducts with their inlets inside the cowling between the cylinders.

The usual indicating devices are in the cockpit to show the position of the undercarriage, the flaps and so forth. There is also a buzzer which goes off if the throttle is closed when the undercarriage is up. All the auxiliary control operating levers are conveniently mounted on the right hand side of the pilot's seat.

No mention may be made of the armament or bomb-load, but normally the crew consists of three men — a pilot, a bomb-aimer-navigator and a radio-operator gunner.

Bristol's latest Blenheim

From The Aeroplane, *November 2, 1938 (not credited)*

AN IMPROVED BRISTOL BLENHEIM has been specially released by the Air Ministry for exhibition at the Paris Show.

The most noticeable modification is a completely new nose-section which has improved both the appearance and the performance. The figure given as the nominal maximum speed for this latest version of the Blenheim is 295 m.p.h. (524 km.h.). Presumably this is with full load. Under ideal conditions, the modified Blenheim should be considerably faster. All the more so because the standard Blenheim is reputed to be capable of exceeding 300 m.p.h. when pressed.

The all-up weight for the new version has been raised from 12,030 lb. to 14,400 lb. The empty weight has been increased from 7,409 lb. to 8,250 lb. Nevertheless, the disposable load is increased by 1,750 lb. to 6,150 lb.

The result of this is that the range has gone up from 1,125 miles to 1,900 miles in still air when cruising at 220 m.p.h. at 15,000 ft. Two extra fuel tanks of 94 gal. provide the necessary extra fuel.

The new nose affords much better accommodation for the crew than in the original version. It contains a chart table, instruments and a folding seat for navigation and improved bomb-aiming

K7072, in its final guise as the prototype long-nose Blenheim Mk IV. The aircraft had a busy career, being passed through various units including the A&AEE and 48 Squadron, before becoming a pattern aircraft for Rootes. In 1938, the aircraft carried out de-icing and cabin heating trials with the RAE and, on August 15, 1940, K7072 was grounded in preparation for it to be transported to Canada. Based at Rockcliffe, the Blenheim carried out further de-icing trials before it saw out its days with the National Research Council in Canada. (via Martyn Chorlton)

equipment. Because of the special shape and construction of the nose, the crew have an excellent view in most directions.

Another improvement in this machine is the use of 100 octane fuel for take-off. This increases the take-off power of the Bristol Mercury VIII motors from 725 to 920 b.h.p. Thus, in spite of the increased load, the take-off and climb are the same as the standard Blenheim. For normal operation, 87 octane fuel is used as in the standard version of the Blenheim.

The number of the crew and the bomb-loads remain unaltered.

From *Britain First* to Blenheim Mk IV

From The Aeroplane, *January 19, 1940 (not credited)*

One of the most fascinating of abstract pleasures to be derived from aeronautical affairs is watching the evolution of the design of particular types of aeroplane from the first prototype to the latest mark of production model.

Usually this evolution is a story of steady development and advance with an improvement in every quality. Occasionally, the evolution is retrograde and the final production model is inferior to the first conception. This sometimes happens when the machine is converted to fulfil some purpose for which it was not originally designed.

One of the most interesting of recent stories of progress in design and conception of a new technique is that of the Bristol Blenheim, evolved from the so-called Rothermere Bomber, "Britain First," of 1935. Although the Blenheim has descended from what would have been the World's best civil transport when it was built, the conversion has not made it any the less successful as a bomber. In its latest form the Blenheim is still one of the most formidable aeroplanes of its class in the World.

The Bristol Aeroplane Co. Ltd. has believed in the monoplane since its earliest days—and it is nearly 30 years old now. Even when the monoplane was officially frowned on just before the last war, the Bristol company continued in its belief. In 1918, the little Bristol Monoplane single-seat fighter

Bristol's long-serving Chief Test Pilot, Cyril Uwins

Cyril Frank Uwins, OBE AFC

Cyril Frank Uwins was born in Croydon in 1896 and, like so many other young men, answered the call at the beginning of the First World War. He initially served with the London Irish Rifles before joining the RFC in the spring of 1916. He went on to serve as a pilot with 43 and 54 Squadrons before being transferred to Farnborough as a ferry pilot in 1917. At the beginning of 1918 he had formed a brand new flying school at Lake Down, Salisbury Plain followed by a fortuitous posting to No.5 Aircraft Acceptance Park at Filton.

Being at Filton instantly brought him into contact with the Bristol Colonial Aeroplane Company Ltd (later Bristol Aircraft Company Ltd) and by August 1918 he was offered the chance to become a test pilot. The following year, he left the RAF to become Chief Test Pilot for the company, a position he held for a record-breaking 29 years.

From the Bristol Scout through to the Type 170 Freighter, Uwins made an incredible 54 'first flights' including the Type 142, Type 143 and all subsequent Blenheim marks before retiring from flying in 1947. His association with the company did not end there as he was then offered the position of assistant managing director of the Aircraft Division. In 1957, he was promoted still further by becoming the deputy chairman of the company and at the same time was the President of the Society of British Aircraft Constructors during 1956 and 1957.

Cyril Uwins, OBE, AFC passed away in 1972.

The Bristol Blenheim Mk IV

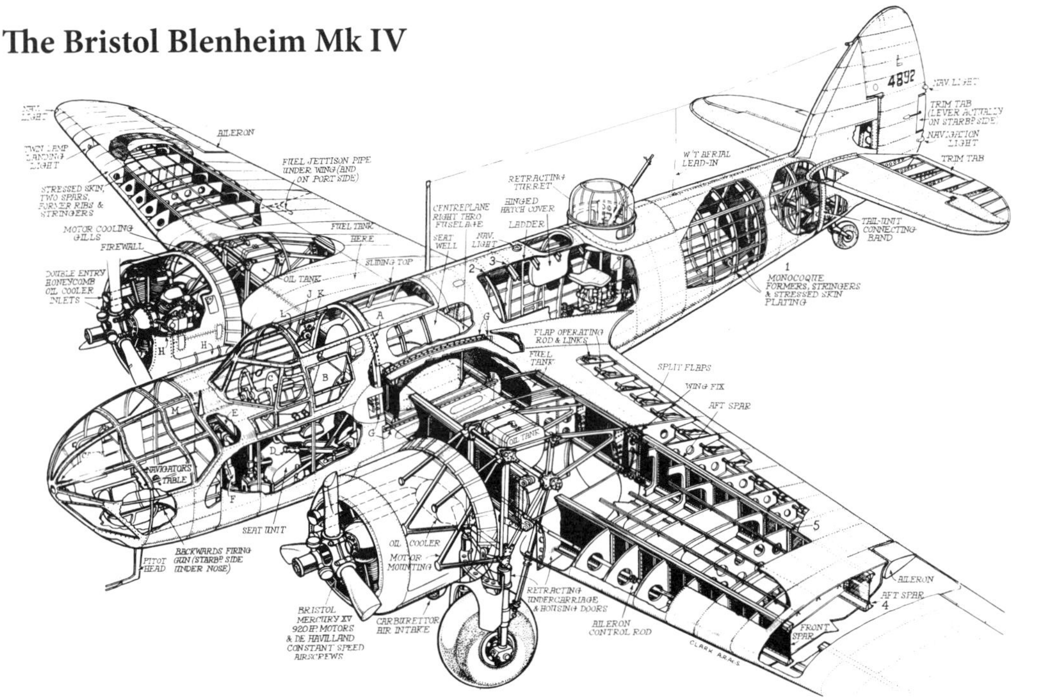

appeared and had both performance and fighting qualities so superior to anything contemporary with it that had it been adopted over the Western Front it might have become one of the most famous aeroplanes of all time. It was ahead of its time and was certainly the best single-seat fighter of the War.

After the War, Bristols continued their monoplane policy in spite of great success with many biplane designs. The soundness of that policy is now evident.

The design of a new all-metal stressed-skin low-wing transport monoplane was first announced by the Bristol Aeroplane Co. Ltd. at the Paris Aero Show in November, 1934. On the Bristol stand, the company exhibited the

Detail view of a Mercury VII and Rotol propeller in an early production Mk IV on December 5, 1938. (*Aeroplane*)

front half of a furnished fuselage—minus tail, wings or wheels. At that time stressed-skin construction and clean lines were so much of a novelty that the Bristol exhibit created quite a sensation. A boom in air transport seemed likely and the Bristol company appeared to have a machine which would lead the field.

Nothing more was made public of this aeroplane until an announcement was made in August, 1935, that it had been bought by Lord Rothermere, christened *Britain First*, and presented to the British Nation as a high-speed bomber. At that time, the Bristol 142, *Britain First*, with two 120 kp. Bristol Mercury VIs, was about the fastest aeroplane in the World, except for machines built for racing. The top speed was around 300 m.p.h.

When the 142 was tested at Martlesham, the reports were so enthusiastic that 200 bombers modified from the type were ordered at once. That was a big order for those days. The modified type, the Bristol 142 M, was called the Blenheim.

The first production Blenheim appeared in the Summer of 1936. The most noticeable alteration from its forebear was the alteration from low to mid wing. The reason for this was more to provide storage for bombs under the spars than for aerodynamic advantage. It formed the star attraction of the Paris Aero Show in November, 1936.

The Bristol Blenheim began a new fashion in fast medium-size two-motor bombers which are at the same time manoeuvrable enough to be used as fighters. The official top speed over the earlier short-nose version of the Blenheim with two 840 h.p. Bristol Mercury VIIIs was given as 285 m.p.h. at 15,000 ft., and the range 1,125 miles at 200 m.p.h. In fact, the Blenheim is faster than this and is known to have exceeded 300 m.p.h. on the level.

The next stage in the evolution of the type was in November, 1938, when—just in time to be exhibited at the Paris Aero Show that year—the new long-nose Mark IV version of the Blenheim was announced. The speed was given officially as 295 m.p.h. at 15,000 ft., the loaded weight increased from 12,500 lb. to 14,400 lb. and the range to 1,900 miles at 220 m.p.h. The longer nose afforded more room for the navigator and bomb aimer and made operations more comfortable.

Although the Blenheim went into service as a fast medium bomber it has since been modified for use as a long-range multi-seat fighter as well. Blenheim bombers took part in the first raid of the War on Wilhelmshaven on September 4. Later, they were used as long-range fighters to attack German seaplanes at Borkum. Blenheims of the Bomber Command have flown thousands of hours on reconnaissance and have photographed the whole of the Siegfried Line.

Bristol test pilot 'Bill' Pegg poses for the camera before taking Mk IV L4842 for a publicity sortie in 1938. The aircraft entered service with 53 (Army Co-Operation) Operation and went missing on May 17, 1940 on a reconnaissance operation looking for enemy troops. (*Aeroplane*)

In the shadow of Uwins – Arthur John 'Bill' Pegg

'Bill' Pegg first joined the RAF in 1921 as an apprentice at the tender age of 15 to train as a flight mechanic. In 1925, he applied and was accepted for pilot training, going on to join 43 Squadron as an NCO pilot. It was not long before his flying ability shone through and, in no time, he was carrying out instructor duties. He was commissioned in 1931 and not long after he was posted to the A&AEE at Martlesham Heath as a test pilot. With a promising career ahead of him in the RAF, Pegg took a different direction and, in 1935, joined the Bristol Aeroplane Company as a test pilot, working under Cyril Uwins. Pegg stayed in this position for another 12 years, becoming Chief Test Pilot in 1947 when Uwins retired. Pegg went on to carry out the maiden flights of the Brabazon and Britannia and, by the time he retired, he had flown 150 different types of aircraft.

Arthur John 'Bill' Pegg passed away in 1978.

L4842 with 'Bill Pegg' at the controls during the Bristol Aircraft Company publicity sortie carried out in 1938. (*Aeroplane*)

Chapter 3

Mass Production for an Expanding Air Force

U p to 1935, aircraft production at Bristol's Filton factory had been a comparatively laid back affair with a steady flow of work providing the RAF with biplane fighters and bombers, the latter being sub-contracted work from Hawkers. When the first order for the Type 142M was received in early 1935, under Air Ministry Contract No. 43506/35 for 150 aircraft, the Bristol Aircraft Company had to raise its game rapidly to meet such a large request. Further pressure was applied as the same contract was accompanied by an 'Instruction to Proceed' which gave the company the go ahead to begin the task of purchasing enough materials for another 450 aircraft.

Having 600 bombers on their order books in a short space of time, and during peacetime, was unheard of and to carry out the work on such an advanced aircraft, a whole new approach would have to be adopted with regard to the 142M's production. All this was happening at the same time as the last Bulldog fighters were leaving the factory and Bristol's commitment to build Audax would not be completed until November 1936. Compared to these 1920s heritage biplanes, the 142M was a cutting

Mk Is as far as the eye can see with engines mounted at Filton in January 1938. In the foreground bottom right the 8½ gallon oil tank needed to keep each Bristol Mercury engine lubricated is exposed. (*Aeroplane*)

Filton 1938. While some workers pause momentarily for the camera, the majority keep working, adding atmosphere to this wonderful production photo. Mk Is and Mk IVs can be seen in an advanced state of assembly with engines and controls being fitted in the Erecting Hall. (*Aeroplane*)

Where metal is skilfully turned into machine. From the rear of the picture the all-metal fuselage takes shape until it becomes one of the major sectionalised semi-monocoque components seen in the foreground. The fuselage has a 'developable' surface which was a period term to describe an external form of fuselage or component, which, although tapering, does not have a double curvature. By avoiding the double curvature large metal sheet panels can be applied without the nead for beating. (*Aeroplane*)

edge 'state of the art' design and would need as many new techniques and improved production efficiencies to build it.

To achieve this, the aircraft was designed in a number of major sections, 15 to be exact, and on August 1, 1935, one of Frank Barnwell's team, Leslie Frise, distributed a memo throughout the drawing office giving details of how this should be carried out. Each major section was planned to be built on its own jig which could be allocated its own section of the factory and which would also allow good access for the engineers. Once completed, each section would then be moved to the main assembly line. Sectionalising the aircraft was a very innovative approach at the time but would set a precedent for virtually all massed produced aircraft from 1935 onwards. Repair and transportation of large aircraft components was also made easier with this method, especially once the bomber entered service.

Filton expands

The 142M was, by far, the largest aircraft to be built at Filton and it was obvious that the company's infrastructure would have to be expanded and brought up to date. There was already a very large Erecting Shop on site which was built in 1916 and had not changed since. The shop was expanded to twice its original size and a taxiway was built directly to it, connected to the airfield's main perimeter track. All of the machine-shops and tool-rooms were expanded and re-fitted with up-to-date machinery.

An early production photo taken at Filton showing the first major batch of 450 Mk Is ordered to Contract No. 527111/36 and 529181/36. Visible amongst the many are L1164 (crashed Sep 3, 1939), L1167 (to 3542M Feb 3, 1943), L1170 (SOC Aug 17, 1943) and L1172 (SOC Jul 24, 1943). (via Martyn Chorlton)

A new, large shop was built just for the production of wings and it included facilities to carry out nickel-plating, anodising and cadmium-plating. Added to this building was a large metal store to cater for the hundreds of tons of Alclad alloy sheeting of varying gauges required for the stresses skin of the 142M. A Press Shop, Assembly, Experimental and Flight Production Departments were also created, not to mention a large cellulose Paint Shop. Such was the amount of new components involved in the bomber that new departments were created for development and production of hydraulic systems including engine pumps for the flaps and undercarriage and the dorsal gun turret.

Being a Bristol-made product, the Mercury engines would also need a host of new facilities of their own. A dedicated 200,000sq ft factory was constructed on the eastern side of the Gloucester Road in an area known as Patchway. This site eventually grew to three times its original size and even in 1935 the Engines Division employed nearly 2,700 people, nearly twice as many as the Airframes Division. Various engine test sheds, experimental and development offices filled the site and an additional plant called the Rodney Works was built just to construct cowlings and exhaust systems.

To generate sufficient revenue to fund all of this expansion, the Bristol Aeroplane Company became a limited company, created a share capital of £1.2 million (approximately £50 million today). By April 1936, part of the revenue raised resulted in the construction of a new 'Filton House' complete with stone reliefs of *Britain First* and a Mercury Engine emblazoned on its modern exterior. This building replaced the original 'old' Filton House which was the converted private house of the founder of the original company (British & Colonial Aeroplane Company), Sir George Stanley White. When Sir George passed away in 1916, his brother Samuel became chairman and his only son, Stanley, became Managing Director. In turn, when the company was reformed as the Bristol Aeroplane Company in 1920, Sir Stanley White became chairman and remained in this position until 1955.

One of two ways of lifting a 1,000lb Mercury engine into place was by the use of a Herbert Morris single hoist, as demonstrated here. (*Aeroplane*)

The design offices were also moved and expanded and a new Technical Office was created, specialising in aerodynamics, airframe structure, stressing and weight estimation. By late 1935, the drawing office alone had 338 staff, which was more than three times the amount being employed by Handley Page at the same time. During the same period, the skilled staff at Filton had expanded from 4,200 to 8,233 compared to a little of 2,000 employees, just two years earlier. The employment figure continued to rise as the Second World War approached and, in October 1939, Bristol had 16,542 skilled employees on its books.

Expansion Scheme F

From the end of the First World War, the RAF was dramatically reduced and, with the Government applying a 'Ten Year Rule', the force had to make do with obsolete equipment for much longer than they were designed to last. The rule simply applied the theory that the government of the day did not foresee a war in the coming ten years and this was the case until the world began to change in the early 1930s.

The first of eight new 'schemes' was approved in July 1934 and was known as Expansion Scheme A, which called for a new front line strength of 1,544 aircraft. Before this figure was reached, the process was superseded by Expansion Scheme C (B never came to fruition) which increased the total number of operational aircraft to 1,804 aircraft. Neither scheme D or E got off the drawing board before the arrival of Expansion Scheme F which was approved in February 1936. This was the scheme

The other method of positioning the Mercury engines was by the double hoist. Again Herbert Morris-built, this twin engine hoist, rated to 4 tons, is used to make the job even easier. (*Aeroplane*)

that the new Blenheim would form the core of and Bristol would significantly benefit from another batch of huge orders. Within scheme F, the number of front line aircraft rose to 2,204, of which over 1,000 were bombers and 240 of them were heavy bombers. The Blenheim at this stage was classed as a medium bomber and it was this part of the scheme that saw the highest increase in strength, rising from 216 to 350 aircraft. On top of this, the new scheme called for a reserve force which was more than double the strength of the front line and this equated to a need for 8,000 new aircraft over a three-year period. To keep up with the demand, the Bristol Aeroplane Company would have to expand its own operations still further and that could mean the introduction of sub-contractors and the arrival of the government sponsored 'shadow factory'.

Mass production

By July 1936, further contracts were signed for the Blenheim Mk I and, by the time the first production aircraft was delivered to 114 Squadron at Wyton in March 1937, it was clear that more plants would be needed to keep pace with the demands of Expansion Scheme F. To meet this need, two other British companies became involved in the production of the Blenheim, the established aircraft manufacturer A.V. Roe at Chadderton and the car manufacturer Rootes Securities based at Speke.

Remarkably, both companies would build more Blenheims than Bristol by the time they had completed their orders. Avro built 1,005 Blenheims between August 1938 and October 1941, by which time the production lines were cleared for the Avro Lancaster. The Lancaster benefited a great deal from replicating the same sectionalised production techniques employed by the Blenheim. Rootes went on to break all Blenheim production numbers by building 3,419 from November 1938 to June 1943. Construction was carried out at its giant shadow factories at Speke and Blythe Bridge, while assembly took place at Meir and Shawbury.

Bristol went on to build 955 of the 6,185 Blenheims constructed and this was probably a good reflection of how quickly the company was moving on to new designs. The Beaufort was already being ordered in large numbers before the outbreak of the war and Beaufighter had already begun production by 1940.

UK Production

One Type 142 ordered by Lord Rothermere in March 1934; delivered to A&AEE June 1935 by Bristol, Filton to Contract 419009/35
K7557 (R-12, G-ADCZ [not carried])

150 Type 142M ('Blenheim' Mk Is from March 1936) delivered between Jan 1937 and Jan 1938 by Bristol, Filton to Contract 43506/35
K7033 to K7182

450 Blenheim Mk Is delivered between Feb 1938 and Mar 1939 by Bristol, Filton to Contract No.527111/36 and 529181/36
L1097 to L1546

34 Blenheim Mk Is delivered between Mar and Jul 1939 to Contract No.529181/36
L4187 to L4822 and **L4907 to L4934**

84 Blenheim Mk IVs delivered between Mar and Jul 1939 to Contract No.529181/36
L4823 to L4906

250 Blenheim Mk Is delivered between Aug 1938 and Mar 1940 by A.V. Roe & Co., to Contract No.588371/36
L6594 to L6843 *(L6696 to L6708 to Romanian Air Force; L6817 to L6819 & L6821 to L6834 to the Royal Yugoslavian Air Force)*

250 Blenheim Mk Is delivered between Nov 1938 and Aug 1939 by Rootes Securities, to Contract No.551920/37
L8362 to L8407, L8433 to L8482, L8500 to L8549, L8597 to L8632, L8652 to L8701, L8714 to L8731 *(L8619, L8620, L8622, L8624 to L8630, L8632 and L8654 to Romanian Air Force)*

130 Blenheim Mk IVs delivered between Sep and Nov 1939 by Rootes Securities, to Contract No.551920/37
L8732 to L8761, L8776 to L8800, L8827 to L8876 and **L9020 to L9044**

220 Blenheim Mk IVs delivered between Nov 1939 and Mar 1940 by Rootes Securities, to Contract No.569202/36
L9170 to L9218, L9237 to L9273 *(all of this batch were originally built as Mk.Is but modified to Mk.IV standard before delivery)* **L9294 to L9342, L9375 L9422** and **L9446 to L9482**

100 Blenheim Mk IVs delivered between Mar and Jun 1940 by A.V. Roe & Co., to Contract No.588371/36
N3522 to N3545, N3551 to N3575, N3578 to N3604 and **N3608 to N3631**

100 Blenheim Mk IVs delivered between Apr and Aug 1939 by Bristol, Filton to Contract No.774679/38
N6140 to N6220 and **N6223 to N6242**

70 Blenheim Mk IVs delivered between Aug and Oct 1939 by Bristol, Filton to Contract No.774679/38
P4825 to P4864 and **P4898 to P4927** *(P4910, P4911, P4915, P4916, P4921 and P4922 registered as G-AFXD, G-AFXE, G-AFXF, G-AFXG, G-AFXH and G-AFXI respectively for the Royal Hellenic Air Force)*

62 Blenheim Mk IVs delivered between Sep 1939 and Jan 1940 by Bristol, Filton to Contract No.774679/38
P6885 to P6934 and **P6950 to P6961**

30 Blenheim Mk IVs delivered in Jun and July 1940 by A.V. Roe & Co., to Contract No.588371/36
R2770 to R2799

R2800 to R2805, R2825 to R2864, R2877 to R2926, R2939 to R2963, R2995 to R3040, R3076 to R3128 and R3140 to R3144 were all cancelled Avro-built Blenheim IVs under Contract No.588371/36

250 Blenheim Mk IVs delivered between Mar and Jun 1940 by Rootes Securities, to Contract No.1485/39
R3590 to R3639, R3660 to R3709, R3730 to R3779, R3800 to R3849 and **R3870 to R3919** *(R3877 to Free French Air Force)*

400 Blenheim Mk IVs delivered between Jun and Oct 1940 by Rootes Securities, to Contract No.1485/39
T1793 to T1832, T1848 to T1897, T1921 to T1960, T1985 to T2004, T2031 to T2080, T2112 to T2141, T2161 to T2190, T2216 to T2255, T2273 to T2292, T2318 to T2357, T2381 to T2400 and **T2425 to T2444** *(T1867, T1875, T1935, T2077 and T2079 to Free French Air Force)*

800 Blenheim Mk IVs delivered between Oct 1940 and May 1941 by Rootes Securities, to Contract No.1485/39
V5370 to V5399, V5420 to V5469, V5490 to V5539, V5560 to V5599, V5620 to V5659, V5680 to V5699, V5720 to V5769, V5790 to V5829, V5850 to V5899, V5920 to V5969, V5990 to V6039, V6060 to V6099, V6120 to V6149, V6170 to V6199, V6220 to V6269, V6290 to V6339, V6360 to V6399, V6420 to V6469 and **V6490 to V6529**

420 Blenheim Mk IVs delivered in July 1940 and May 1941 by A.V. Roe & Co., to Contract B119994/40
Z5721 to Z5770, Z5794 to Z5818, Z5860 to Z5909, Z5947 to Z5991, Z6021 to Z6050, Z6070 to Z6104, Z6144 to Z6193, Z6239 to Z6283, Z6333 to Z6382 and **Z6416 to Z6455**

430 Blenheim Mk IVs delivered between May and Nov 1941 by Rootes Securities, to Contract No.B1485/39
Z7271 to Z7320, Z7340 to Z7374, Z7406 to Z7455, Z7483 to Z7522, Z7577 to Z7596, Z7610 to Z7654, Z7678 to Z7712, Z7754 to Z7803, Z7841 to Z7860, Z7879 to Z7928 and **Z7958 to Z7992**

Z7993 to Z8002, Z8050 to Z8099, Z8143 to Z8167, Z8202 to Z8236 and Z8274 to Z8323 all cancelled

200 Blenheim Mk IVs delivered in May and Oct 1941 by A.V. Roe & Co., to Contract B119994/40

Z9533 to Z9552, Z9572 to Z9621, Z9647 to Z9681, Z9706 to Z9755 and **Z9792 to Z9836**

Z9886 to Z9935 & Z9949 to Z9978 all cancelled

Two Blenheim Mk V prototypes originally named 'Bisley' by Bristols, Filton to Contract B.69276/40
AD657 and AD658

Five Blenheim Mk IVs built by A.V. Roe & Co., to Contract B.1485/40
AE449 to AE453 (no record of delivery or service for this batch)

110 Blenheim Mk Vs delivered between Nov 1941 and Jan 1942 by Rootes Securities, Speke and Blythe Bridge and assembled at Meir and Shawbury to Contract B1485/39
AZ861 to AZ905, AZ922 to AZ971 and **AZ984 to AZ999**

669 Blenheim Mk Vs delivered between Jan 1942 and Jun 1943 by Rootes Securities, Speke and Blythe Bridge and assembled at Meir and Shawbury to Contract B1485/39
BA100 to BA118, BA133 to BA172, BA191 to BA215, BA228 to BA262, BA287 to BA336, BA365 to BA409, BA424 to BA458, BA471 to BA505, BA522 to BA546, BA575 to BA624, BA647 to BA691, BA708 to BA757, BA780 to BA829, BA844 to BA888, BA907 to BA951, BA978 to BA999, BB100 to BB102 and **BB135 to BB184**

Two Blenheim Mk V prototypes delivered by Bristol, Filton in Sep 1941
DJ702 and DJ707

160 Blenheim Mk Vs delivered between Dec 1942 and Jun 1943 by Rootes Securities
EH310 to EH355, EH371 to EH420, EH438 to EH474 and **EH491 to EH517**

EH518 to EH533, EH550 to EH581, EH599 to EH634, EH651 to EH700, EH718 to EH749, EH763 to EH796, EH802 to EH831 and EH848 to EH872 all cancelled

Canadian production
626 Blenheim Mk I, IV, IVW, IVC and IVT built by Fairchild Aircraft Ltd, Longueil, Quebec
Mk I **702 to 719**
Mk IV **9001 to 9004, 9006 to 9009, 9024 to 9073** and **9075 to 9201**
Mk IVW **9005** and **9010 to 9023**
Mk IVC **9074**
Mk IVT **9851 to 10256** (*plus 51 spare airframes*)

Yugoslavia production
16 Blenheim Mk Is built and another 24 destroyed before completion by Ikarus A.D., Zemun. 20 Blenheim Mk IVs; components sent to Finland

Finland production
65 Blenheim Mk I and IV built by Valtion Lentokonetehdas, Tampere
Mk I **BL146 to BL190**
Mk IV **BL196 to BL205** (*BL191 to BL195 not assembled*)

The main manufacturers
- **The Bristol Aeroplane Company Limited** based at Filton (Bristol)

- **Avon** (Mk I, Mk IV and Mk V prototypes)

- **Alexander V. Roe (Avro) Aircraft Company Limited** based in Greengate, Middleton (Chadderton), Lancashire (Mk I and Mk IV)

- **Rootes Securities Limited** at Blythe Bridge (Stoke-on-Trent), Staffordshire (Mk IV and Mk V)

- **Rootes Securities Limited** at Speke (South Liverpool), Lancashire (Mk I and Mk V)

- **Fairchild Aircraft Limited** in Longueil, Quebec, Canada (Bolingbroke)

- Also built under licence by **Valtion Lentokonetehdas** (State Aircraft Factory) at Tampere, Finland (Mk I and Mk IV)

- **Ikarus AD** in Belgrade (Zemun), Yugoslavia (Mk I).

Chapter 4

"With Speed I Strike"

The history of 114 Squadron begins in 1917, in RFC days, when it was formed on September 22 from two flights of 31 Squadron at Lhore, India. The squadron initially operated a rag-tag collection of BE.2Cs, Henry Farman F.27s and BE.2Es in an effort to suppress troublesome tribesmen. These air demonstration operations were carried out until March 1918 and from later that year the squadron split itself between Quetta and Lahore with another flight in Aden. By October 1919, the squadron had received the capable F.2B Fighter but by April 1, 1920 had lost its identify after being renumbered as 28 Squadron.

Arrival of the world's fastest bomber

After being disbanded following the First World War due to the shrinking RAF, 114 Squadron was revived again on December 1, 1936 as part of a new expanding air force under the command of Sqn Ldr H Hamilton-Brookes. Reformed as a bomber squadron at Wyton, the weapon of choice was the Hawker Hind, followed briefly by the Audax, but both were only a temporary measure as the squadron was earmarked for 'the fastest bomber in the world'.

It was March 1, 1937 when the sound of a pair of Bristol Mercury engines was heard over Wyton for the first time. The first aircraft was K7035, modified as a dual control trainer, followed three days later by K7036, K7037 and K7038 as part of a delivery of 12 aircraft. The Blenheim was the first aircraft in RAF service to feature an all-metal monocoque monoplane design, retractable undercarriage, wing flaps, variable pitch propellers and a power-operated turret. This was a major leap in technology and there was a sudden increase in performance which many pilots took a while getting used to after the Hind.

114 Squadron's pristine Blenheim Mk Is during exercises in the summer of 1937. Both K7043 and K7045 survived squadron service to become instructional airframes at Henlow and Cranwell. (*Aeroplane*)

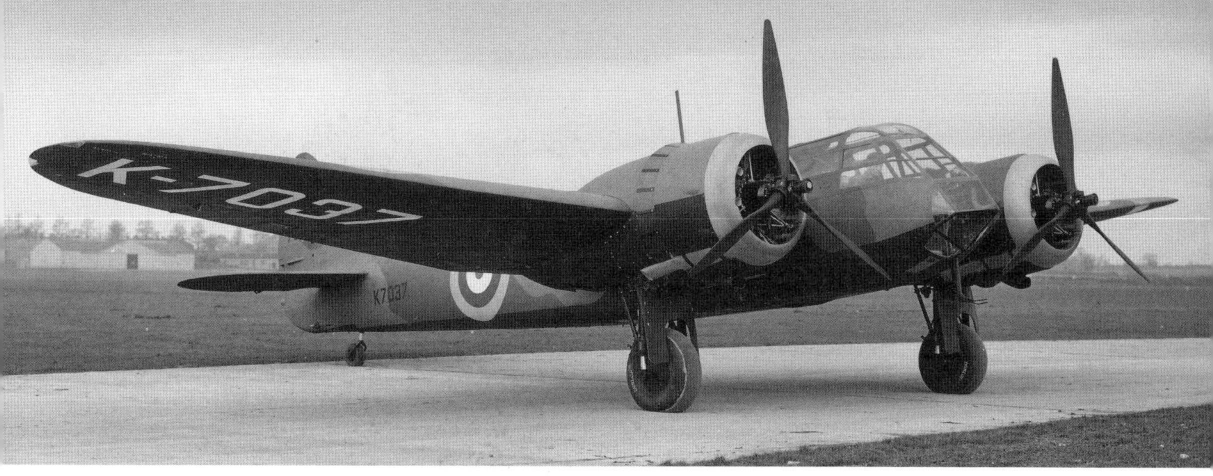

K7037 was one of three aircraft delivered to 114 Squadron on March 3, 1937. After more than 12 months of trouble-free flying, disaster struck on May 5, 1938 when an engine cut on take-off from Wyton. Sadly, the Blenheim crashed on the edge of the airfield killing all three crew. (via Martyn Chorlton)

It was not long before one pilot got caught out by the Blenheim, much to the chagrin of the CO. On March 10, an unnamed pilot had just carried out a high-speed pass in K7036 over a gathering of personnel from the squadron. After banking hard, the flaps and undercarriage were lowered before he made his approach and subsequent landing. All was going well until the pilot gave the powerful hydraulic brakes a tad too much pressure. The tail suddenly rose, and before the unfortunate pilot had chance to correct his error, the propellers had dug into the grass, sending the Blenheim onto its back. While the pilot escaped with only his pride battered, K7036 was beyond repair and was SOC (Struck off Charge) on June 8 with just two hours of flying time under its belt. K7036 was replaced by K7057 which was delivered on June 18 and, ironically, this aircraft was destined to become the squadron's second loss when it crashed during a night landing at Wyton on September 30 after the pilot became disoriented.

114 Squadron's record was not an untypical example of the number of accidents that occurred as pilots grappled with both the new technology and the new world of high-powered asymmetric as

The first significant incident to occur after the arrival of the first Blenheims at RAF Wyton, was the destruction of 114 Squadron's first aircraft. K7036, which was only delivered on March 4, 1937 lies wrecked on the edge of Wyton with its back broken. (via Martyn Chorlton)

The spine of K7036 was broken as it toppled over after the brakes were applied a tad to hard. The bomber had flown for a total of just two hours. (via Martyn Chorlton)

engines failed at crucial moments. 114 Squadron was destined to lose ten of its Blenheims before the beginning of the Second World War including a Blenheim Mk IV, the first of which began to join the unit from May 1939.

On a lighter note, the squadron were the star attraction at the 1937 RAF Pageant at Hendon. Part of their display was a very close three-ship formation which passed low over the massive crowd. The public got close to the Blenheim on the ground for the first time as well. The pageant was cancelled the following year because of events building overseas, namely the 'Munich' crisis, but this did not stop the Blenheims performing at Hendon again in 1939 only weeks before the world was plunged into war again.

Prior to this, the Blenheim squadrons were heavily involved in home defence exercises and manoeuvres, including a trial designed to 'discover the effect of air attack on dispersed aircraft' in September 1938. 114 Squadron was one of several units involved in the trial which involved 30 SOC Bulldog fighters with full fuel tanks, tethered on a 1,000yd in diameter dummy airfield. Incendiary ammunition was also dispersed out into the open, providing a tempting target to the attacking Blenheims. The first attack by six Blenheims took place from 2,000ft with 72 40lb GP (General

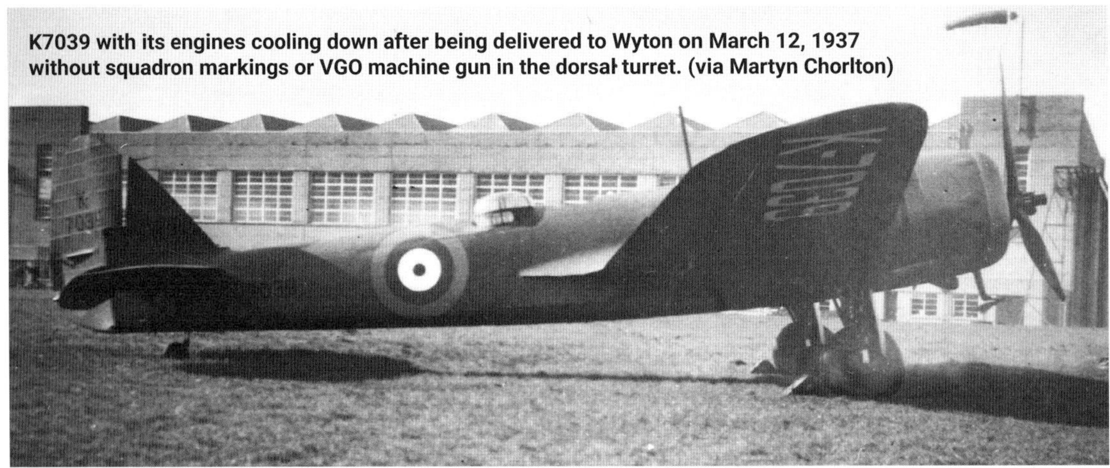

K7039 with its engines cooling down after being delivered to Wyton on March 12, 1937 without squadron markings or VGO machine gun in the dorsal turret. (via Martyn Chorlton)

Above: An informal line of 114 Squadrons which must have been taken before April 1938. The reason for this is that K7041, pictured second in this line up, was DBR (Damaged Beyond Repair) on April 4, 1938 when an engine cut and the Blenheim was forced to make a belly landing on the airfield. K7046, nearest the camera gave good service to 114 Squadron until March 16, 1936 when it was given Maintenance No.1329M and saw its days out with 1 EWS. (*Aeroplane*)

Right: 114 Squadron's very own 'V for Victor' featured in one of the many Bristol adverts which were prevalent throughout the late 1930s. (*Aeroplane*)

Purpose) bombs but, after leaving craters between 50 and 200yds from the nearest Bulldog, no damage was caused. Half-a-dozen more Blenheims followed with 24 250lb GP bombs from 2,000ft, attacking a group of Bulldogs parked in protective pens. Craters were left within 30yds of the pen but, once again, little damage was caused. Finally, another six Blenheims came down to 1,000ft dropping a salvo of 250lb bombs but the majority broke up on impact or did not go off.

Embarrassingly, it a took a flight of nine Fairey Battles, armed with 36 250lb GP bombs and instantaneous fuses to straddle a line of the old fighters, destroying three and damaging at least two more. The ineffectiveness of the Blenheim in these controlled conditions against a target that was not even firing back was very worrying.

War declared

On September 3, 1939, Britain was at war and, while a certain amount of confusion and chaos ensued within the ranks of the RAF, a pre-arranged plan involving 1 Group's Battles being sent to France and 2 Group's Blenheims being dispersed around the British countryside was put into action.

For 114 Squadron, which was now part of 82 Wing, 2 Group, it meant being dispersed to Hullavington. Behind, at Wyton, 139 Squadron, which had converted to the Blenheim in July 1937, flew the RAF's first operational sortie of the Second World War, a reconnaissance sortie looking for capital ships. 114 Squadron, among others, were waiting for the results of the reconnaissance, with

K7040 'V' pictured en route from Filton to Wyton on March 22, 1937. (*Aeroplane*)

nine Blenheim Mk IVs loaded with SAP (Semi Armour Piercing) bombs ready to attack the enemy ships. By the time the recce Blenheim had landed the light had been lost but the squadron would remain at readiness during these early days of the war.

France

Once the initial expectation of the imminent arrival of the Luftwaffe appearing over British soil had subsided, 114 Squadron re-congregated at Wyton. The squadron would now be involved in the war in a different way, and before September was over, a single Blenheim was sent to Rheims on detachment. In October, three more were sent to Villeneuve-les-Vertus and, by this stage, it was looking more likely that 114 Squadron would be heading for an overseas posting. It was from Villeneuve that 114 Squadron flew its first operation of the war when two Blenheims took part in a reconnaissance of the Ruhr area. One aircraft managed to carry out the sortie successfully but the other aircraft, Blenheim Mk IV N6160, failed to return. It is presumed that the bomber either succumbed to flak or to enemy fighters resulting in Plt Off K G S Thompson, Sgt G S Marwood and AC2 A Lumsden becoming the squadron's first operational casualties. A combination of poor weather and pilot error also resulted in six more killed when N6145 and N6150 collided during a reconnaissance sortie of Heligoland on November 11.

In the meantime, Wyton became very busy as two AASF (Advanced Air Striking Force) Battle squadrons arrived from France to re-equip with the Blenheim. To replace these two units, both 114 and 139 Squadron were sent to France, the former arriving at Condé/Vraux on December 9, 1939. Prior to this, both squadrons had been withdrawn from operations in November and their Blenheims stripped and repainted using Titanine with the undersides painted a pale 'sky blue' as developed by Sidney Cotton's PDU at Heston.

During March and April 1940, the squadron was detached to Perpignan/La Salanque from where it continued to fly reconnaissance operations, returning to Condé/Vraux on May 10. The following day, the squadron had a taste of what the Luftwaffe could really do when the airfield was attacked by nine Do 17Zs of 4./KG2 at 0545hrs. Six Blenheims Mk IVs were destroyed on the ground, virtually eliminating the unit before it had a chance to take part in the Battle of France proper.

On May 14, just two serviceable Blenheims took part in 114 Squadron's first bombing operation of the war as part of 75 Wing at 0855hrs from Condé/Vraux. The operation was an armed reconnaissance of the Sedan, Givonne and Bouillon area which resulted in a German MT column being attacked in the village of Bosseval. One of the pair involved, L9464, was shot down at Glaire-et-Villette killing the three crew, Plt Off C B Jordan, Sgt P M Southwood and

Unusual view of the pilot (left) and navigator/observer of a 114 Squadron Mk I, taken by the air gunner, from behind the rear spar. (*Aeroplane*)

One of the six 114 Squadron Blenheims destroyed on the ground at Condé/Vraux on May 11, 1940 by the Luftwaffe.

LAC T W Brown. It was a grim day for 2 Group and the RAF as a whole, with 47 light bombers destroyed, 14 of them Blenheims and the remainder Battles.

By 1200hrs on May 18, what remained of 114 Squadron prepared to evacuate to Nantes before returning to England. The remaining aircraft regrouped at Crécy where they were transferred to 18 Squadron, the rest of squadron not reaching Nantes until May 21. The bedraggled and dejected remnants finally arrived at Wattisham at 1145hrs on May 31, 1940.

A 114 Squadron Blenheim MK IV abandoned at Condé/Vraux in June 1940.

Back with Bomber Command

After moving again to Horsham St Faith on June 10, 114 Squadron began to find its feet again as new aircrew and aircraft began to arrive. The new impetus was kept moving by 2 Group as a whole which, by now, could boast up to 180 Blenheims for its daily operations; three times more than it could deploy in France a few weeks earlier.

It was now time for 114 Squadron to play its part of the Battle of Britain which was not just fought over south eastern England. Priority targets were now the channel ports and enemy airfields, the vast majority of these being attacked in broad daylight, with only cloud providing any cover. The squadron were back in action by early July, including a daylight raid on the 5th against Soest airfield in Germany. Plt Off A Stewart's crew in R3804 were the only loss, the first since their mauling in France.

Having moved to Oulton three days earlier, 114 Squadron responded to Hitler's Aldertag by bombing, for the first time, the only part of British soil occupied by the enemy. The airfield on Jersey was the target and 114 Squadron despatched 17 Blenheims to bomb it. Results are not known but one Blenheim, L9265, flown by Plt Off I T H Carson, failed to return.

Losses continued to mount for 114 Squadron with a further nine Blenheims lost before the end of 1940, resulting in another 16 crew killed and five injured.

Mk IV 'RT-L' being inspected by Germans at Condé/Vraux in June 1940.

Action photo, taken during the attack on the Knapsack power station, on August 12, 1941. Sgt I Brooms aircraft, V6391 'RT-V' can be seen turning away from the target.

The first 'Circus'

Devised in late 1940, 'Circus' operations were designed to encourage the Luftwaffe fighters into battle by despatching a relatively small bomber force, escorted by a very large force of RAF fighters. The very first RAF 'Circus' operation took place on January 10, 1941 from Hornchurch with 114 Squadron providing six Blenheims, led by the CO Wg Cdr G R A Elsmie, and 72 fighters (three squadrons of Hurricanes and three of Spitfires) from 11 Group providing a hefty escort. Another 24 Hurricanes flew on ahead to strafe St Inglevert airfield while the target for the Blenheims was a German ammunition dump at Forêt de Guines, south of Calais. Very few hits were recorded on target but 114 Squadron all returned safely and, on this occasion, the Luftwaffe did not rise to the bait.

114 Squadron flew its second 'Circus' with six Blenheims on February 5, in the company of six more from 139 Squadron. They attacked the airfield at St Omer. Nine managed to bomb the target and all of the Blenheims returned home safely but this time the Luftwaffe were up for the fight, shooting down nine Allied fighters for the loss of just one Bf109. From 114 Squadron's point of view, 'Circus' operations were a 'piece of cake' compared to the unescorted daylights and night bombing operations over Holland and Germany.

On loan to Coastal Command

Shipping losses during early 1941 had reached crippling levels and, in an attempt to stem the flow, Bomber Command lent several squadrons to 18 Group Coastal Command. 114 Squadron was one of the units chosen, moving to Thornaby on March 2 to carry out convoy escort, anti-submarine and anti-shipping patrols.

These types of operations always involved spending hours over the very uninviting North Sea, often without seeing any sign of the enemy, although they were occasionally relieved by strikes on targets in Norway, such as the ports of Aalborg and Bergen. Attacks on enemy shipping were a rare event for 114 Squadron and, up to mid-April, the unit had escaped any serious losses. However, on

Operation Archery was declared a success, achieving its overall aim of keeping as many German troops in Norway as possible.

April 18, this was all about to change when three Blenheims, led by the CO, Wg Cdr Elsmie AFC in R3837, spotted five enemy vessels off the Norwegian coast.

As the flight dived to attack, they were bounced from astern by several Me110s which sent all three aircraft crashing in flames into the sea, with the loss of another nine valuable aircrew. Matters did not improve the following day when Sgt B Beardsley in R3806 crashed on take-off and all three on board were killed after the bomb load exploded. A similar waste of life occurred on April 28 when, after returning from an uneventful convoy patrol, V6022, flown by Plt Off J G K Long, crashed two miles short of the safety of Thornaby's runway. Once again, three more Blenheim aircrew were killed.

The costly attack on the Knapsack power station did not stop Bomber Command from attacking the plant at least two more times before the end of the war. However, it was never attacked in broad daylight and at low-level ever again.

Down to just ten serviceable Blenheims, 114 Squadron moved further north to Leuchars on May 13, still under 18 Group control. The same routine of convoy escort work was continued, although encounters and attacks on enemy Merchant Vessels (MV) were on the increase, often with mixed results. Four Blenheims joined 42 Squadron's Beauforts on the night of July 10/11 in an attack on Sola airfield which resulted in something for 114 Squadron to shout about. Several fires were started in the target area and all returned safely back to Leuchars.

Two nights later, 114 Squadron joined 42 Squadron again, this time with nine Blenheims on a strike against German Naval Forces. The target was undoubtedly the *Lützow*, which was first spotted by Sgt Staples in 'W' of 114 Squadron just before midnight on July 12/13 after the Blenheim attempted to attack an enemy float plane off the Norwegian coast. Losing the enemy aircraft after flying into heavy rain, the crew of the Blenheim emerged in clear air not far from four to five enemy destroyers, which were screening a 'much larger warship', described as 'probably a cruiser'. Two hours later, a Beaufort of 42 Squadron delivered a crippling blow to the cruiser *Lützow*, putting the cruiser out of action until May 1942.

On July 19, 1941, 114 Squadron's tour of duty with 18 Group was over and the unit flew south to West Raynham, to return to the 2 Group fold.

Operations *Sunrise* and Knapsack

Barely settled in at their latest Norfolk home, 114 Squadron were called upon to support a long-planned major daylight raid against German warships in Brest harbour on July 24 called Operation *Sunrise*. 2 Group's Blenheims would play a diversionary role in the raid by despatching 36 Blenheims, in several waves, in an attack against the docks in Cherbourg. Despatched in three waves, all with Spitfires providing escort, the final wave was made up of

A dramatic series of photos taken from a rear facing camera of a 114 Squadron Blenheim Mk IV as they sweep across the Luftwaffe airfield at Herdla on December 17, 1941.

12 114 Squadron Blenheims led by the CO, Wg Cdr G L B Hull. From a raid point of view, the attack was a success with considerable damage caused to the dock area, although the flak batteries were well awake by the time 114 Squadron was over the target – at least three Blenheims were damaged. Unfortunately, the attack was unsuccessful as a diversion and did not draw any enemy fighters away from the main attack which suffered very high losses. It was clear that Bomber Command could not operate effectively in daylight.

The daylight operations continued for 2 Group and they pushed their luck even further with a daring raid deep in Germany against the Knapsack and Quadrath/Fortuna power stations near Cologne on August 12, 1941. The object of the exercise was to try and draw as many Luftwaffe fighters as possible away from the Russian front despite the fact that Fighter Command could only provide an escort that stopped a long way short of Cologne. Fifty-four Blenheims were organised for the raid, split into two waves, one of 38 aircraft to attack Knapsack (including 12 of 114 Squadron led by Wg Cdr Nicol) and 18 to Quadrath. The raid was the first for the squadron's new CO but his observer, Flt Lt T Baker DFM, was described as the best navigator in 2 Group and this is where the bulk of the

Bombs burst across Herdla as a single Bf109 attempts to take off from the snow covered runway.

responsibility lay if the raid was to be a success. Loaded with two 500lb bombs each, the Blenheims set course for Germany at 0950hrs and, formatting at just 100ft, rendezvoused with their fighter escort near Martlesham Heath. As the formation approached the Scheldt estuary, the fighter escort climbed to 1,000ft but, in what seemed a very short period of time, the fighters had to turn for home. The Blenheims then came down to just 50ft, literally hedge-hopping and only climbing for power lines all the way to the target. One Blenheim fell victim to power lines en route, two were shot down and V6197, a 114 Squadron aircraft had to abort. The remaining 50 Blenheims swept as fast as they could towards their targets, delivering all of their bombs accurately on the two power stations. Flak poured from all directions and two more Blenheims were brought down but, up to now, 114 Squadron had escaped with just flak damage. Unfortunately, five more aircraft were lost on the way home, including Z7281, flown by Sgt D J Wheatley, which was hit by flak and crashed into the Westerschelde off Vlissingen. The raid was immediately declared a success and even the BBC and the press gave the operation almost legendary status. 2 Group played it down, stating quietly that they had got off lightly despite the fact that 10 aircraft were lost to flak or fighters, equating to an unsustainable loss rate of 18.5%.

Anti-shipping patrols were on the agenda again from late August 1941 onwards but, compared to those flown from Scotland, 114 Squadron was now flying them in the more hostile territory of the Channel and off the Belgian and Dutch coasts. One such operation claimed the life of the CO, Wg Cdr Nicol DFC on August 19 when, despite having fighter escort, three of 114 Squadron Blenheims were shot down into the sea off the Dutch coast by enemy fighters of 5./ZG76. Out of the nine airmen involved that day, only the air gunner of V6366, Sgt A Clague, survived to become a PoW. It was a similar story on October 15 when six 114 Squadron and six 139 Squadron Blenheims carried out another attack on shipping off the Frisian Islands. 5./ZG76 were the victors again, shooting down two Blenheims of 114 Squadron and four from 139 Squadron; there were no survivors and another alarming loss rate of 42% was the result. It was a dreary period for the Blenheim and 2 Group, a period that saw 27 Blenheims from 110 and 114 Squadrons shot down during anti-shipping operations with only one of the 81 airmen missing known to have survived. It was clear that the role was not suitable for the Blenheim and, much to the relief of those involved, the last anti-shipping operation was flown on November 2. The wartime figures of attacks present 590 ships bombed with over 200 of them claimed as sunk or badly damaged since March 14, 1941. Post-war research reduced the actual number down to 50 vessels, 29 of which were sunk and 21 damaged. 2 Group alone lost 139 Blenheims against shipping and coastal targets.

Operation *Archery*

The final major operation of 1941 was also the first of many 'Combined Operations' and saw 114 Squadron heading back to Scotland, this time even further north to Lossiemouth. Operation *Archery* was a combined operation to test German forces in Norway and convince their senior staff that an invasion of the country was on the cards. Planned for December 17 1941, the Blenheims of 110 Squadron from Wattisham and 114 Squadron arrived the previous day. The objective was Vågsøy Island and six Blenheims from 110 Squadron and 13 from 114 Squadron, led by Wg Cdr Jenkins, were detailed to take part. The whole operation hinged on the lead navigator, Flt Lt P Brancker, who successfully navigated the entire 300 mile flight by dead reckoning.

As the attack began, the 110 Squadron Blenheims attacked shipping in the Oberstad area to draw away German fighters from the main commando assault. 114 Squadron's job was to attack, at low-level, the Luftwaffe fighter airfield at Herdla. This was skillfully carried out but the success was marred when V6227 and Z7500 collided over and crashed onto the airfield, killing all six aircrew. The operation was classed as a huge success having achieved all of its objectives but once again Bomber Command had paid a high price, losing eight of 29 aircraft dispatched, six of them being Blenheims.

114 Squadron, along with 82 and 110 Squadrons, were made available by 2 Group in support of Operation *Fuller* on February 12, 1942. The objective was to stop the *Prinz Eugen*, *Gneisenau* and *Scharnhorst* from escaping from Brest. Unfortunately, the weather favoured the enemy and all managed to escape, under the noses of the RAF and Royal Navy.

New leader, new policies, new role

With the arrival of Air Marshal Sir Arthur Harris, at the helm of Bomber Command from February 22, 1942, the role of 2 Group was summed in one of his early dispatches, '… this short-range force could play no part in the main offensive against Germany.' Harris was obviously right, it was the job of his mediums and heavies, not the lightly armed Blenheims risking life and limb on daylight operations. The honour of flying 2 Group's last daylight operation fell to 114 Squadron, when Wg Cdr Jenkins led six Blenheims on an escorted attack against the submarine pens at Ostend February 28; all returned safely to West Raynham. 2 Group was now preparing for massive re-equipment program as the long overdue types such as the Boston, Ventura, Mosquito and Mitchell gradually crept into service while they continued to play a major part in the training role.

It was not quite over for 114 Squadron, as Harris was well aware that the Blenheim still had a useful role to play as a night intruder against enemy airfields. These operations were still very dangerous, although the benefit of operating at night at least gave the Blenheim crews more opportunity of making a surprise attack. The intruder operations also became equally useful as a diversionary tactic, a good example being on the night of March 26/27, when 104 bombers attacked

Mk IV V5468 of 114 Squadron, one of the 34 Blenheims of 2 Group that took part in the first 1,000-raid on May 30/31, 1942

Essen after various diversions took place, including 11 114 Squadron Blenheims to airfields in Holland. It was another costly night though and two more Blenheims, Z7307 and Z7700, fell to the guns of Ofw P Gildner of II./NJG2 following an attack on Soesterberg; both aircraft crashing with the loss of all six aircrew into the Waddenzee, north of Wieringen. The following night, 114 Squadron was in action again while the famous St Nazaire raid was taking place, eight Blenheims went intruding over Holland. The

Intruder crew. Sgt G Shackleton (right) and his observer preparing to leave West Raynham for an intruder operation.

night brought another body blow to the squadron, when Wg Cdr J F G Jenkins DSO, DFC and his experienced crew of Flt Lt P Brancker DFM and Flt Sgt C H Gray DFM, were all killed after Z7276 was hit by flak during a raid on Soesterberg.

Only three weeks later the squadron's latest commanding officer, Wg Cdr G L B Hull, who had returned for second tour of duty, was flying an intruder to Schiphol airport in Z7440 when the Blenheim was damaged by light flak on April 17/18. Luckily, Hull managed to crash land near Aalsmeer without injury to his crew but were destined to spend the rest of the war in captivity.

Losses were comparatively light during April, with V5458 lost over Leeuwarden on the 24/25 and Plt Off J R N Molesworth RAAF having a very eventful sortie on the 26/27. After bombing Eindhoven in T2420, the Blenheim was badly shot up by a Ju88 on the return flight. Relieved to escape the attentions of the Luftwaffe, on crossing the Suffolk coast, a 'friendly' anti-aircraft battery opened up on them, damaging the bomber still further forcing Molesworth to crash land at Pulham. All on board were injured but at least they had survived.

The first of Harris' 1,000 bomber raids took place on May 30/31 and, once again, 2 Group, including 114 Squadron were called upon to provide a healthy 34 Blenheims for attacks on night fighter airfields. While the giant raid pummelled Cologne, two Blenheims were shot down including V5645 flown by Plt Off J J Fox RNZAF. His two crew were killed in the initial impact, and although Fox survived the initial crash he had died by June 1. The squadron was also in action during the second 1,000 bomber raid against Essen on June 1/2. 48 Blenheims from 2 Group were detailed to attack German airfields but only ten actually made any attempt to attack and three were shot down. Once again it was 114 Squadron that came out worst losing Flt Sgt B P L'Hirondelle RCAF and crew in R3620 and V6337, flown by Sgt J L Mitchell and crew. The latter, after bombing Venlo airfield, was hit by flak and crashed into the English Channel. The third and final 1,000 bomber raid on Bremen June 25/26 was also contributed to by 114 Squadron, with their efforts split between the main target and the airfields at Ardorf and Leeuwarden.

Intruder operations continued throughout June and July with attacks on Bonn, Vechta, Venlo, Twente, Ardorf and Leeuwarden were all bombed for the loss of three more Blenheims and their nine aircrew. Some of these operations were flown from Lossiemouth again but, by August 1942, the pace began to slacken as the Blenheim finally, and not before time, began to take a back seat within Bomber Command.

In early August, the squadron was detached to Wigtown as part of Exercise Dryshod which was a dress rehearsal of the forthcoming raid on Dieppe. Aircraft began to leave West Raynham from August 3, including R3813, being flown by Plt Off A J Hicks. Whilst over Cheshire, the Blenheim suffered an engine fire and, during the pilot's attempts to carry out an emergency landing at Hawarden, the bomber crashed at Lacha House in Chester. All three crew and one ground engineer, AC1 G Craddock, were killed marking the last 114 Squadron Blenheim Mk IV loss whilst serving with Bomber Command.

The Blenheim Mk V and Operation *Torch*

In early November 1942, 114 Squadron began to re-equip with the Blenheim Mk V, well aware that they had been chosen along with 13, 18 and 614 Squadrons to move to North Africa in support of Operation *Torch*. On November 13, the squadron's air component left West Raynham and, after flying via Portreath and Gibraltar, they arrived at Blida on November 15. The previous day the squadron had lost two Blenheims en route. BA826 flown by Sgt A Johnson and crew force landed at Lisbon Airport and after being interned were later released to the UK. The other loss was BA750 which ran out of fuel and was forced to ditch near Tangier, resulting in Plt Off W Walker and crew also being interned. On arrival, the four Mk V squadrons came under the control of 326 Wing, commanded by Gp Capt L Sinclair GC. The wing was assembled to support the British 1st Army, who were advancing towards Tunisia, with attacks on airfields and any enemy positions, convoys or supply dumps and ports. 114 Squadron were in action fairly quickly, losing its first aircraft in action on November 23 when Plt Off J Mathias and crew failed to return from an attack on Sidi Ahmed.

The ground crews alone were operating under very primitive conditions and it was not long before the aircrews also discovered that the Blenheim Mk V was not up to the conditions, let alone the task demanded of it. Accidents claimed more Blenheims than the enemy as the Mk V, thanks to its increased weight, could not fly on one engine, despite the efforts of the ground crew who removed the extra armour and rear firing guns in an attempt to lighten the aircraft.

On December 5, 326 Wing moved to Setif with detachments operating from Canrobert which was 150 miles closer to the front. By December 17, the wing was permanently established at Canrobert, an airfield that would be its home for several months to come. Daylight raids were first carried out with fighter escort, but these began to tail off during the winter months as the airfield began to deteriorate.

Losses were mounting for 114 Squadron throughout the remainder of December with five more aircraft destroyed in action or accidents. These were comparatively light compared to 13 and 18 Squadrons who had lost 55 Mk Vs between them leading up to the beginning of 1943.

Considering the amount of operations flown by 114 Squadron from January April 1943, the squadron lost 8 more aircraft, only four of them in action, before the unit began to convert to the Douglas Boston Mk III after over six years of operating the Blenheim.

The Commanding Officer of 114 Squadron, Wg Cdr J F G Jenkins DSO, DFC (third from left) who was killed on March 27, 1942. His crew that day, Flt Lt P Brancker DFM (second from right) and Flt Sgt C H Gray DFM (right), were also killed.

114 Squadron's post-Blenheim years

The Boston saw out the war years for 114 Squadron and remained on strength until the unit was renumbered as 8 Squadron in Aden in September 1946. Reformed in Egypt in August 1947 with Dakotas, the role of routine air transport was carried out throughout Middle East Command. The Valetta took over in 1950 and in March 1956 the squadron was moved to Cyprus, where it was disbanded late in 1957. Re-formed yet again in December 1958, the squadron carried out the unique task of flying Chipmunks from Nicosia on anti-EOKA patrols before it was disbanded again in March 1959. On May 5, 114 Squadron was revived again at Colerne, once again in the transport role, this time with Hastings which were operated until it was disbanded again on September 30, 1961. The following day, the squadron was reformed again in preparation for becoming the first RAF unit to operate the Argosy, the first of which did not arrive until late February 1962. As the Argosy came to end of its operational service, 114 Squadron was disbanded for the final time on October 31, 1971.

114 Squadron reformed for a fifth time in April 1959 but was only destined to operate the Hastings C.1 and C.2 (seen here) until September 1961. (via Martyn Chorlton)

The units sixth and final re-incarnation came in October 1961 when 114 Squadron became the first to operate the Armstrong Whitworth Argosy. (via Martyn Chorlton)

Chapter 5

The Home Defence Exercise

The following article is from the *Aeroplane*, August 10, 1938, by C. M. M. A.

After several years, during which the Air Defence Exercises have been held only on a very limited scale because of reorganisation or overseas commitments, a full-scale Exercise was held this year from August 5 to 7.

The main objects of the Exercise were to train the air and ground defences of Great Britain against air attack. The Exercise had no political significance and the area of the operations was chosen for economy and convenience.

This operational area was within the line Humber, Dover, South London, Andover, Evesham, Leamington, Rotherham, Humber thus affording protection to the industrial centres of the Midlands and on the outskirts of London – see map.

In the past, major air defence exercises have been planned in connection with the defence of London, but the expansion of the RAF and the large increase in the strength of the ground units which operate under the control of the Fighter Command have allowed the area to be extended this year.

The Fighting Services are, traditionally, reluctant to interfere with civil liberties even when they are engaged in schemes for the protection of the civil population, but this year the Air Staff were forced, in the interests of safety, to curtail civil flying within the area of the operations.

War games. A map of the 'playing field' for the Home Defence exercise of August 1938 showing the area of operations and the locations of the fighter, attacking and friendly squadrons. (*Aeroplane*)

FAST BOMBERS – Bristol Blenheims being re-fuelled after a raid. Because of the hot weather the airmen were allowed to work in their shirt sleeves. The waist-belts on the gas-mask harness are to keep the packs out of the way of men working on aeroplanes. (*Aeroplane*)

Mk I K7058 of 90 Squadron prepares to leave Bicester on a single bomber raid. K7058 had a long and eventful career including at least two occasions when the undercarriage collapsed while serving with 2 SAC at Andover. By mid-1942, after passing through several different units, the Blenheim saw out its days with the RAE until SOC on December 4, 1943. (*Aeroplane*)

THE RAIDER - A Bristol Blenheim coming in to land after a raid. In the foreground is a sand-bagged machine gun post for the defence of the aerodrome. (*Aeroplane*)

They were particularly sorry to have to interfere with some of the small joy-riding companies whose existence, they appreciate, depends to some extent on the business they can do at the height of the Summer.

Apart from this, the Exercise was held without any inconvenience to the civil population. The Air Raid Precautions Department of the Home Office co-operated to some extent, in that they used their warnings organisation, but any 'black-out' which may have inconvenienced the public were entirely local efforts. Those local authorities who used the Exercise to practise a black-out and any other A.R.P. practice showed commendable enterprise.

Those who have followed the Air Defence Exercises since they were first made public in 1927 will appreciate the broad and elastic lines on which Home Defence against air attack has been built. Co-operation between the Services and with the civilian element is on the best possible foundations. The Air Force, the anti-aircraft guns and the searchlights, together with the Observer Corps, work together with enthusiasm and with an ever-increasing regard for each other's abilities.

In the opinion of the Air Staff, expressed by a distinguished Officer at a conference at the Air Ministry on August 3, the object of the Home Defence organisation is to increase the percentage of interceptions of enemy air raids. The Air Staff will not be satisfied until the interceptions are 100 per cent, and even that will not defend the Country adequately unless the interceptions inflict heavy losses on the enemy.

To do this we must always have a fighter superior to the enemy's contemporary bomber in performance and in hitting power. We have this in our new eight-gun fighter, but we must keep, not one jump, but two jumps, ahead of enemy bombing tactics and bombing material.

The speaker said that about Home Defence he was an optimist. Home Defence succeeds by inflicting heavy losses on the enemy, and heavy losses mean that his approaches are limited to darkness and bad weather. He, personally, disliked the exaggerated importance paid to putting on gasmasks and sleeping in cellars but, because no one can guarantee that a proportion of enemy bombers will not get through the defences, proper precautions must be taken to minimise casualties when they do get through.

He might have added with some justice that successful and efficient A.R.P. is likely to be of considerable help to the combatant side of the defence organisation.

Air strength

The Exercise this year was of special interest because of the large increase in the strength of the units involved both in the air and on the ground and because of many other features which were new to a Major Exercise.

The number of aeroplanes used in the Exercise was 925, more than double the number which has taken part in any previous year. Also, nearly all these machines were of the post-expansion period – in other words they have been brought into service since 1935. And they do not by any means cover the total strength of the Metropolitan (or Home) Air Force.

The ground forces employed were two Anti-Aircraft Divisions and seven complete and two incomplete Groups of the Observer Corps.

The Defending Force, known as Westland, consisted of 23 fighter squadrons, 14 bomber squadrons, two anti-aircraft divisions and the Observer Corps. Its total strength in aeroplanes was 450. The whole force was under the command of Air Chief Marshal Sir Hugh Dowding, G.C.V.O., K.C.B., CMC, A.D.C, Air Officer Commanding-in-Chief, Fighter Command, and the units were:

Nos. 3, 19, 23, 25, 29, 32, 41, 46, 54, 56, 64, 65, 66, 72, 73. 74, 79, 85, 87, 111, 151, 213, 601 and 604 (Fighter) Squadrons; Nos. 9, 21, 37, 38, 49, 50, 75, 83, 99, 107, 115, 149, 214, and 215 (Bomber) Squadrons; the 1st A.A. Division, T.A., the 2nd A.A. Division, T.A.; and Nos. 4, 11, 12, 15, 16, 17, 18 and parts of Nos. 31 and 19 Groups of the Observer Corps.

The fighter squadrons were stationed at Northolt (2), Duxford (3), Wittering (3), Debden (4), Biggin Hill (3), Digby (2), Hornchurch (3), North Weald (3) and the bomber squadrons of Stradishall (1), Waddington (2), Feltwell (2), Marham (2), Scampton (3), Honington (2) and Mildenhall (2).

The ground forces were disposed about the operational area in positions which may not be disclosed.

The Attacking Force, known as Eastland, consisted of 36 bomber squadrons with a total strength of 475 aeroplanes under the command of Air Chief Marshal Sir Edgar Ludlow-Hewitt, K.C.B., C.M.G., D.S.O., M.C., Air Officer-Commanding-in-Chief, Bomber Command. The units were:

Nos. 7, 10, 12, 15, 18, 35, 44, 51, 52, 57, 58, 61, 62, 63, 76, 77, 78, 82, 88, 90, 98, 104, 105, 108, 114, 139, 142, 144, 207, 218, and 226 (Bomber) Squadrons, and Nos. 206, 217, 220, 224, 233, and 269 (General Reconnaissance) Squadrons.

They were stationed at Finningley (2), Dishforth (2), Andover (2), Abingdon (1), Upper Heyford (2), Cottesmore (2), Bicester (2), Linton-on-Ouse (2), Upwood (2), Hemswell (2), Cranfield (2), Driffield (1), Boscombe Down (2), Hucknall (1), Bassingbourn (2), Harwell (2), Wyton (2), Bircham Newton (2), Tangmere (2) and Gosport (2).

The operations should have been continuous for 48 hours with all the units concerned in action throughout, including the Observer Corps, which, in previous years, has shut down during part of each night. Also, in other years there have been intervals during which certain units of the Service ground defences were not working. But the weather interrupted.

This year, for the first time, the anti-aircraft gun command and communications were in full operation.

The Balloon barrage was taken into consideration this year although no balloons were flown. But certain areas were assumed to be covered by balloon barrage and any formations which flew through these areas were assessed by the umpires as having lost one machine in four.

Friendly bombers

The inclusion of friendly bombers among the units of the defending force was to give the defending force, air and ground, training in recognition so that, in time of war, the defences will be less likely to attack their own bombers and to prevent loss of working hours in important industries caused by false air raid warnings. Because this recognition training is in the elementary stage, the friendly bombers were all of types, different from those of the attacking units.

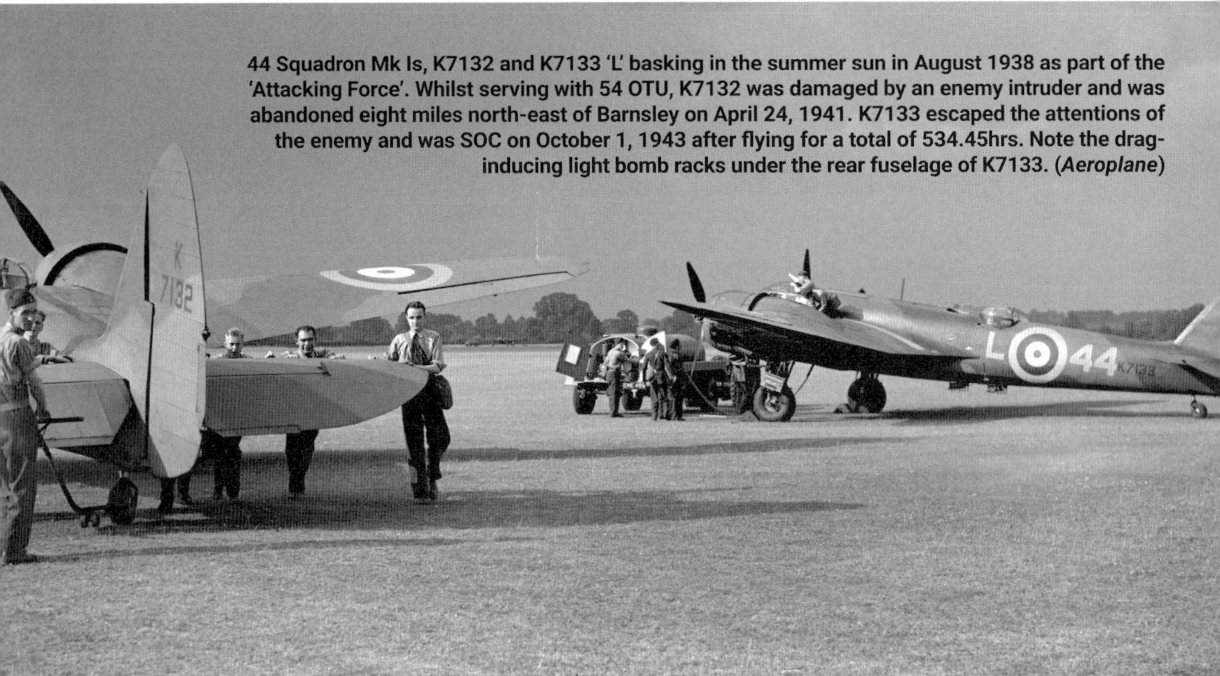

44 Squadron Mk Is, K7132 and K7133 'L' basking in the summer sun in August 1938 as part of the 'Attacking Force'. Whilst serving with 54 OTU, K7132 was damaged by an enemy intruder and was abandoned eight miles north-east of Barnsley on April 24, 1941. K7133 escaped the attentions of the enemy and was SOC on October 1, 1943 after flying for a total of 534.45hrs. Note the drag-inducing light bomb racks under the rear fuselage of K7133. (*Aeroplane*)

Nice viewpoint of Mk I K7067 'B' of 90 Squadron at Bicester. Only weeks after this photo was taken, the Blenheim was abandoned after control was lost in icy conditions over Cottonhopehead Moor, near Redesdale Camp in Northumberland. (*Aeroplane*)

But the most important new feature this year was the number of new types of aeroplanes used. The crews gained experience in operating their machines under approximately active service conditions and the greatly increased speed of the machines presented new problems to the ground forces and demanded new tactics from the fighters.

Apart from these features, the Exercise was more or less on the plan of previous Exercises. The attacking force was employed in operations against military targets with reasonable freedom of action by subordinate commanders.

Enemy formations were allowed to go to their targets, in spite of having been intercepted or roughly handled by the fighters and ground defences, so that as much training as possible could be given to the defence.

Fighters had to make as many interceptions as possible and the ground forces had to observe, locate, and fire at hostile bombers and, at the same time, avoid taking action against friendly aircraft.

The sky limit

No operations were allowed below 4,000ft. within seven miles of London Bridge. All fighters had to use navigation lights at night and bombers had to turn on their navigation lights if there was any possibility of collision. No aeroplane was allowed to approach within 300yds of an opponent and fighters were not allowed to attack bombers below 1,000ft.

A special weather organization was in operation to provide regular forecasts and a signalling organization was ready to give help to aeroplanes should bad weather develop during the Exercise.

Spectators may have watched the raids and thought that an undue proportion of attacking aeroplanes was getting through the defences. The explanation is that not only were the bombers allowed to go on their way uninterrupted because of the need for training the defences but in real war the most important part of the defences would be the striking force which would have attacked military objectives in the enemy country, destroyed some of the enemy before they left home and kept a good proportion of the rest at home in defence of their own strategical centres.

The official line

Official reports on the progress of the Exercise issued by the Air Ministry revealed certain facts which link up the reports of our separate observers.

The operations were postponed from 1000hrs until 1400hrs on August 5 because of bad weather. At 1400hrs, the weather was still poor and the Eastland plan had to be modified. Nevertheless, 50 raids were made on Westland and some of them were intercepted by fighter squadrons. The Defence Force bombers also made 20 raids between 1800hrs and 2000hrs.

The plan for mass attacks was altered to attacks by single machines and small formations because of weather but these attacks, mostly on Midland towns by fast medium bombers, were highly successful.

Many raids were cancelled during the night because of fog and others were ordered to return. At 0830hrs on August 6 operations were again suspended until 1400hrs.

Of the raids between 1800hrs and 2000hrs, two-thirds were declared to have been intercepted. A raid by 22 Fairey Battles soon after 1700hrs bombed the Secretary of State for Air and members of the Staff who were visiting Hornchurch.

The Air Minister moved on to Fighter Command Headquarters where he was again attacked by three Whitleys. This formation was attacked and destroyed by a formation of Hurricanes from Northolt.

During the same period, 30 Blenheims from various Stations attacked Bassingbourn, Cranfield and Wyton and the railway cutting at Great Rissington and 11 Battles bombed Abingdon and Harwell.

The Secretary of State visited the Observer Corps and sent them a message of appreciation of their valuable work.

During the night of August 6-7 (Saturday-Sunday), London was the object of a succession of attacks by single machines. At 0130hrs, the fog became general and the bombers were recalled. The fighters went on until 0450hrs to exercise the searchlight units.

114 Squadron keep it tight during one of many simulated raids during the Home Defence exercise. (*Aeroplane*)

139 Squadron on parade at Wyton in 1937. (via Martyn Chorlton)

Three of the Demon two-seat fighters were caught in the fog and, after flying till their petrol was exhausted, the crews abandoned their machines and landed safely by parachute. The pilot of a fourth Demon tried to land at Digby and crashed in a field near the aerodrome. The crew was unhurt.

A Harrow of No. 37(B) Squadron crashed in attempting to land in a field near Bishop's Stortford and the five members of the crew were killed. A Battle of No. 88(B) Squadron also crashed in Essex and one of the crew was killed. The pilot was slightly injured and the other member of the crew was unhurt.

Operations were resumed at 1200hrs on August 7 but heavy rain spread over the whole area, so the machines were recalled and the Exercise cancelled at 1415hrs.

The official report ends in the following words, "Throughout the period of the Exercise the weather has been bad and several postponements have been necessary. Despite this handicap, the Fighter Squadrons, Searchlights, and Observer Corps of the Westland Defence organization have been thoroughly tested and many valuable lessons have been learned.

"The Bomber forces have been operating and taking every advantage of the weather conditions both by day and by night and the crews have obtained practice under warlike conditions."

To which we would add that the RAF was harassed by weather, harried by the super-efficiency and enthusiasm of the Searchlights, and handicapped by its brief experience of its new equipment. Many of them were engaged on an Exercise for the first time and the Exercise was the biggest that has ever been attempted in this country. And they put up a very fine show indeed.

In East Anglia

Service aerodromes are now almost as numerous in the Eastern counties of England as they were in the 1914-18 war and they are far bigger and better equipped. The wide stretches of level country are excellent for flying, particularly in these days when the majority of pilots are inexperienced.

Whether the policy is sound which builds huge permanent air stations on the East side of England where they can be easily seen and attacked is a matter of opinion, and there are many who think that the permanent stations should be in the West with advanced landing fields and refuelling stations in the East.

Advanced landing grounds were not used in these Exercises but they were simulated by the dispersal of the aeroplanes round the edges of the aerodromes. At some Stations, the organization for taking the crews, fuel and ammunition out to the advanced landing grounds was practised although in fact the transport took them only to the other side of the aerodrome.

DEBDEN: Four fighter squadrons were operating from Debden, Nos. 25, 29, 85 and 87, of which No. 85 has only just been formed and No. 25 is not normally stationed there. The Debden squadrons had just finished a week of strenuous co-operation with the Anti-aircraft units in the neighbourhood when the Exercise began. The guns and searchlights arrived from their home stations on the previous Sunday and went out to their posts on the Monday. The rest of the week before the main Exercise began was spent in concentrated practice.

The enthusiasm of some of the searchlight units was so great that as many as ten or eleven searchlights would be concentrated on one unfortunate fighter, which made life very difficult. Actually, the rule is that no more than three searchlights are to concentrate on one target; and if some of the searchlight commanders could have some experience of being in a fighter with more than three lights on him he would not allow his enthusiasm to run away with him again.

All the interceptions from Debden were done by formations of three machines but only one machine did the actual attack. Which machine of the three was to make the attack was arranged before taking off, so that no R/T was used in the air to disclose the position of the formation.

The fighters knew very little about the progress of the operations. They get their orders to go up to a certain level in a certain sector and they either find and engage the enemy or they miss him and come back. The machine which makes the attack comes back on its own anyhow and does not try to pick up the rest of the formation.

STRADISHALL: Although there are two squadrons at Stradishall and they were both there, only one, No.9, was doing any flying with its Heyfords. No.148 is in the process of re-arming and its personnel were doing the ground work of the Station.

Stradishall was opened last March, but the buildings are more advanced than many stations opened earlier.

With plenty of personnel to spare, the ground organisation and Staff work at this station were very impressive. Air raid and gas attack warnings were frequent and machine-gun and other defence posts were manned and gas-masks put on with great alacrity in spite of the oppressive heat of the day.

The Heyfords were part of the friendly bomber forces, which means that they belonged to the Defence Force. This made them a welcome target for attacking bombers, and in less than an hour there were five attacks on the aerodrome; some were by single machines and some by formations of three.

All the attacking machines were Blenheims and the single machines came in low down and had been and gone out of the haze almost before the warning could be given. A earnera-obscura [camera obscura?] out on the aerodrome recorded the result of the raids but some of the raiders carried cameras as well.

Unless warnings come from outside sources, aerodromes have very little chance of defending themselves against such fast machines as Blenheims unless the weather is very clear.

No. 9 Squadron was doing night raids by single machines and the first was not due out until 21 hours. In real war there would have been no Heyfords left to go, after the enemy attacks of the afternoon, nor would the aerodrome have been serviceable. The personnel should, however, have been intact.

View taken from the 'seat well' between the Blenheims two main spars of the pilot and navigator/observer showing just how cosy it was in the front of a Mk I. (*Aeroplane*)

The well-photographed 'V' of 114 Squadron returns to base after another successful 'raid' in August 1938. (*Aeroplane*)

FELTWELL: This was another station of friendly bombers operating at night. There are two squadrons of Harrows at Feltwell, Nos. 37 and 214. They were the first squadrons of this Force to take off for night operations and started leaving, one at a time, every ten minutes at 1830hrs.

Each machine had a course and targets to take about five hours and, as the course took them 80 miles out to sea before coming in to attack, every machine carried a collapsible boat to accommodate the five members of the crew. One squadron was operating seven machines and the other nine.

This station had also been subject to intensive enemy attack from high and low levels before the units were due out.

The machines of both squadrons had the same objectives, Tunbridge Wells and Hawkinge. They went out to sea off Orfordness, crossing the coast at 2,000ft and then climbed to about 9,000ft. They came in again over various parts of the coast, coming down again to 2,000ft for the benefit of the Observers and attacked the targets from 6,500ft.

They were picked up by searchlights between Southend and Chelmsford but saw no fighters and only one or two other bombers. As friendly bombers, these machines were not subject to attack had there been any fighters available and they flew with navigation lights on the whole time.

Friendly bombers were given targets so that they should not lose the opportunity of training.

The weather was good over the targets and on the coast, but visibility was bad over Norfolk and Suffolk. A large area of these counties was blacked out and the crews could not see Newmarket, Cambridge, Ely or any of the main towns in the area. Atmospherics interfered with the radio and one or two were temporarily out of touch with their Station.

The weather was so bad that the machines were all recalled at midnight and the second runs over the targets were cancelled. At midnight, with three machines still in the air, the Station sent up Very lights and other fireworks at five-minute intervals. These were seen nine miles away and helped to guide the machines in. They would have been equally useful to enemy raiders.

Each machine carried two pilots, a navigator, a wireless operator and a rear gunner. Air Vice-Marshal Evill, Air Officer in charge of administration, Bomber Command, travelled in one of the machines.

WYTON: The War was called off at midnight on August 5 and resumed at 1400hrs on August 6, by which time the weather had cleared a little. During the morning, the wind had been between 2 and 5 m.p.h. at ground level and only 15 m.p.h. at 5,000ft, which did nothing to disperse the low cloud and haze.

The two squadrons at Wyton, Nos.114 and 139, both have Blenheims. They did high-level attacks on industrial towns in the Midlands and lower-level attacks on aerodromes. In these Exercises all the low attacks were made on aerodromes to avoid annoying the civil population.

The Wyton squadrons were working with single machine raids the first day up and down a lane assigned to them and out to sea ten miles. Each raid came in from the sea, shot up an aerodrome, bombed a town, went out to sea again, and attacked two more targets before returning.

On the second day, the squadrons took off by flights and joined up with other squadrons in a mass attack on Peterborough and Birmingham.

In a low attack on Mildenhall single machines went out to sea, climbed to 15,000ft and then came onto the target in a long dive, attacking at speed which would leave very little chance for the defenders.

There were 16 single raids on the first day and each machine covered 700 miles during a raid. Some of the attacks were recorded by camera and others by position and stop watch. No one of the 16 raids were intercepted, nor did the raiders see one fighter in the air.

BASSINGBOURN: This new Station, just North of Royston, is occupied by two squadrons, Nos.104 and 108(B) Squadrons. They are being re-armed and were operating with one flight each.

On the afternoon of the second day they were raiding by flights on targets on the industrial towns in the Midlands.

They were subject to anti-aircraft fire between Coventry and Birmingham and heavy rifle fire over St. Ives but saw no fighters. They saw concentrations of anti-aircraft guns near Birmingham, Coventry, Wittering, Leicester and Great Yarmouth. They saw one Hurricane taking off from Castle Bromwich aerodrome but otherwise no fighters in the air, although they could be seen on the ground at Wittering.

The weather was good for evasion but bad for low bombing, and very thick over the industrial towns, where the smoke could not get away. Over these targets the formations broke up and attacked independently. The sea was totally obscured.

Somnambulations

Masterly inactivity, while ready for any sort, size or description of raid, from ground-strafing to gas-spraying (gas understood), was the general impression one got from a tour of some of the Defence Stations and units, between 2100hrs and 0300hrs at the end of the first day and beginning of the second day of the Air Exercises.

Low cloud and bad visibility, with thick fog on the Lincoln Ridge, up until midnight cut down the amount of flying and hampered the defences. In a real war such weather would be the answer to the raider's prayers. But Air Exercises are for the good of all and advantage of none, so bad weather is bad luck. We drove up the Great North Road in spattering rain and turned East at Baldock.

DUXFORD: The first sign of a war or a suggested war was the purple glow from the shaded windows of the Guard Room at Duxford Aerodrome. Obviously few raids were expected because we had not seen a single searchlight all the way up.

The Station Commander took us for refreshment to the luxurious Mess, where past and future raids were being discussed by a perspiring Staff, it was a hot night.

At Duxford there was a tale of early mists, down to the level of the hangars and 10/10 cloud which had delayed the start of operations till 1400hrs. After that a number of raids had come over. Most of them had been made to run the Gauntlet. The Blenheims had made the Gauntlet run very fast.

The defenders thought that more raids had been intercepted than not. They were particularly pleased with the interception of some Blenheim formations. Although the Gloster Gauntlets are some 40 or 50 m.p.h. slower than the Bristol Blenheims they had sat up well above the level of the raiders and dived upon them as they cruised peaceably past. The result had been 30 or more camera-gun photographs and those Blenheims officially in the bag.

Chapter 6

Frank Barnwell and His Work

From the *Aeroplane*, August 10, 1938. C. G. Gray's period text.

Captain Frank Sowter Barnwell OBE, AFC. (*Aeroplane*)

Frank Barnwell was beyond question one of the best aeroplane designers in this country or in the World. No other designer has turned out so many first-class aeroplanes which have become historic.

He and his brother Harold, who belonged to a good old North Country family, were educated at Fettes. They learned engineering together on the Clyde, and that Clydeside training together with their natural ability made them two of the most knowledgeable and useful men in the early days of British aviation. Together they built a big biplane in Scotland in 1908 and got it to running along the ground and hopping. They crashed it in 1909.

When flying really began in this country Frank Barnwell went to the Bristol Company as an engineer and Harold Barnwell went to Vickers Ltd. as a pilot. Harold was a great deal more than a pilot, for his suggestions were generally embodied in the designs of the machines. He was killed during the War while flying a high-speed single-seat pusher biplane at Joyce Green. His death was attributed to his having fainted in the air and having fallen on the controls, for he was known to be unwell.

Frank Barnwell's first outstanding success as a designer was the Bristol Bullet, a little biplane with a Gnôme motor, which was the Bristol answer to the historic Sopwith Tabloid. There was little, if anything, to choose between the performances of the two machines.

Somewhere about that time Frank Barnwell told me that his ideal of an aeroplane was the smallest possible machine with the biggest possible motor, and that idea stayed with him.

At the outbreak of war in 1914 he was already an officer in the R.F.C. Reserve and went to France with the historic first four squadrons but he was soon hauled back to produce better and better aeroplanes.

In 1916 he designed the Bristol Fighter with the Rolls-Royce Falcon motor of 250 h.p., which was admitted by friends and enemies alike to be one of the very great aeroplanes of the War. It had a fine performance for its power, it was extremely manoeuvrable and because the pilot and the gunner were close together back-to-back it gave them more than did any other aeroplane coherence as a team.

As flown during the War it was one of the safest aeroplanes in the World but after the War when it was used for Colonial work and was loaded up with all kinds of unnecessary gadgets it developed a bad habit of stalling and spinning, until it was fitted with slots by an enlightened Director of Technical Development. Nevertheless, it remained one of the greatest of war machines.

V6088 wearing the codes of 13 OTU. Previously the aircraft had served with 86 Squadron and 3 SGR before arriving at Bicester. V6088 was one of the last Blenheims to serve with 13 OTU, being SOC on March 13, 1944. (*Aeroplane*)

Also about 1916, Frank Barnwell produced the Bristol monoplane fighter. Everybody who flew it on active service still holds that it was the best single-seat fighter of the War. It was about the plainest and most straightforward aeroplane that anybody could have designed. And its excellence lay largely in its simplicity. It was in fact as near as Frank Barnwell could go to the biggest motor with the smallest aeroplane.

It was never used in France because the decision about its use fell into the hands of a well-meaning officer who was not a good pilot and found the machine beyond him. Consequently, the few which were built were mostly sent to the Middle East, where they gave the RAF definite superiority in fighting machines over the Turks.

Shortly after the War, Capt. Barnwell produced a most interesting machine which was never taken as seriously as it should have been. It was a single-seat high-wing monoplane. By unbolting the tail unit immediately behind the pilot's seat another section could be bolted in, which consisted of a gun turret with a cantilever monoplane wing below it. The tail unit was then bolted on again behind that.

The idea was that nations which could not afford a large Air Force could buy a number of these machines and could use them either as high-speed single-seat fighters or as heavily staggered two-seat fighters or reconnaissance machines. It was an excellent idea.

Another aeroplane which Capt. Barnwell designed shortly afterwards was a low-wing monoplane completely streamlined and rather the shape of an elongated egg. The undercarriage retracted completely into the belly. With modifications it ought to have been extremely fast.

In 1921, he went to Australia for two years as a Squadron Leader R.A.A.F., to teach the new Service something on technical organisation, but came back to Bristol.

For some time, the Bristol Company's chief activities in aeroplanes consisted of modifications of the Bristol Fighter and a number of very good but not particularly distinguished experimental types were produced until, some ten years ago, the famous Bulldog single-seat fighter was produced, described by a famous pilot as 'The most ladylike machine that ever happened.'

**Bristol M.1C Monoplane.
(via Martyn Chorlton)**

Then, about four years ago, the Bristol Company sent to the Paris Show an all-metal fuselage for a low-wing two-motor cantilever monoplane, evidently hoping that some foreign Power would be more intelligent than the Air Ministry of the period, which had not hastened to order the type.

Just about that period, Lord Beaverbrook had bought an American all-metal monoplane, so Lord Rothermere, not to be outdone, and evidently to show greater patriotism, ordered one of these Bristol monoplanes for himself. Later on he presented the machine to the Air Force which, so far as I have been able to discover, has never used it. It has, I believe, been used as a test machine by the Bristol Company. But at the time of the deal it was much advertised as 'the Rothermere bomber', designed to His Lordship's ideas and presented by him to the nation.

From that type Frank Barnwell proceeded to design a middle-wing monoplane, which is now being used in large quantities by the Royal Air Force and is called the Blenheim. It is, I believe, the fastest twin-motor machine in any Air Force. Its true top speed is not published but everybody knows that the official top speed is a great deal below it.

The Blenheim is an aeroplane of which Frank Barnwell had every right to be proud. In its own line it does represent the smallest possible aeroplane with the biggest possible power plant for its size. So at any rate Frank's friends may claim that his last achievement was worthy of him at his best.

Frank Barnwell was one of the most charming people one could meet. I have known him for 27 years and I have never seen him angry. I have seen him peevish with stupid people in authority, and he always had a gently humorous outlook on a World which he very rightly regarded as being populated

Bristol F.2b Fighter, the 'Bris-Fit'. (via Martyn Chorlton)

Bristol General Purpose Monoplane. (via Martyn Chorlton)

Bristol Type 32 Bullet. (via Martyn Chorlton)

by a bigger proportion of fools than even Carlyle imagined. But unlike most clever people he suffered fools, if not gladly, at any rate tolerantly and with a properly Christian spirit.

Frank Barnwell was fortunate in having the great Bristol Company to back his experimental work. And because he was not hampered by false economy he had better chances of success than many clever men have had. Very rightly his opinions were regarded by his contemporaries with respect. He seldom made speeches, but when he spoke at an Aeronautical Society meeting or anything of that sort he always talked sound sense and always in that pleasing half-serious way which was far more impressive than the impassioned rhetoric of others.

Captain Frank Sowter Barnwell O.B.E., A.F.C., was killed on August 2 while flying at Bristol (Whitchurch) Airport in a small low-wing monoplane (Barnwell B.S.W Mk I G-AFID) which he had had built for his own amusement at the airport. It had a Scott Squirrel motor, of the sort with which various people tried to make Poux de Ciel fly. According to reports, he took off from the aerodrome, got up 100 feet and then dived into the ground.

He had built the little aeroplane in which he was killed purely for his own amusement. For once, he had departed from his old pet theory of having the biggest possible motor. He regarded it more or less as a joke and as a youngster would regard a favourite toy. But he certainly did not regard it as a serious contribution to aeronautical science. The pity is that such a valuable man should have been killed by a plaything. But such things do happen.

**The Bristol Type 72
Racer at Filton in 1922.
(via Martyn Chorlton)**

**Bristol Type 91A Brownie.
(via Martyn Chorlton)**

Captain Frank Barnwell

From The Aeroplane, August 31, 1938

Bristol's long serving designer, Frank Barnwell whose life was cut short on August 2, 1938. (*Aeroplane*)

AT THE INQUEST at Bristol on August 25 on Captain F. S. Barnwell, chief designer of the Bristol Aeroplane Co., who was killed on August 2, Mr. Herbert Cleaverley, an engineer of Airwork Ltd., who made to Capt. Barnwell's design the aeroplane in which he was killed, said that Capt. Barnwell had flown the machine for the first time on July 17 for about six minutes. At that time it seemed to be flying in a semi-stalled position. Capt. Barnwell later made alterations to the 28 h.p. Scott Flying Squirrel motor. It was the only aeroplane that he knew of which was flying at that time with such a low-power motor.

Mr. G. M. Slade, chief flying instructor of the Bristol and Wessex Aeroplane Club, said that on its last flight the aeroplane climbed slowly and then dived from about 70 ft.

Mr. R. C. Hockey, Air Ministry Inspector of Accidents, said that there was no structural failure and that the motor was all right. Capt. Barnwell's flying log book showed that he had made his first flight in 1915 and he had since flown for a total of 485 hours. During the past five years he had only flown for 31 hours. Therefore Capt. Barnwell could hardly be called an experienced pilot.

This strikes us as an unjustifiable reflection on the memory of a very good and experienced pilot. The Air Ministry only requires a few hours a year annual practice from Reserve pilots, and a man of Frank Barnwell's intelligence and experience would need far less.

The verdict was of accidental death. Possibly the reason for the accident was that Capt. Barnwell, unused to such low power, pulled up the aeroplane too steeply, stalled it, and had not sufficient height and power to recover from the dive which followed. Or perhaps the motor stopped or slowed down.

Tragic footnote

Frank was no stranger to the dangers of early aviation. Back in 1917 he lost his brother Harold who was killed test flying the prototype Vickers FB.26 Vampire night fighter which crashed at Joyce Green, Kent on August 25th.

Frank and his wife Majorie later had three sons, Richard, John and David, who despite losing their father in such tragic circumstances all joined the RAF at the beginning of the Second World War. Sadly, their still grief-stricken mother had to endure their losses one by one as all three were later killed on operations. Plt Off John S Barnwell fell first after crashing into the Channel during a night patrol in Blenheim Mk IF L6636 of 29 Squadron on June 19, 1940. Flt Lt Richard A Barnwell was the pilot of Whitley V P5082 of 102 Squadron on the night of Oct 28/29, 1940. After taking off from Linton-on-Ouse, the bomber set course for Bremen and, after signalling that the target had been successfully attacked, the crew set course for home. Unfortunately, the Whitley crashed into the North Sea, 20 miles east of Aberdeen and killed all five on board. Finally, on October 14, 1941, the surviving son, David, also lost his life when his 607 Squadron Hurricane crashed not long after taking off from Manston.

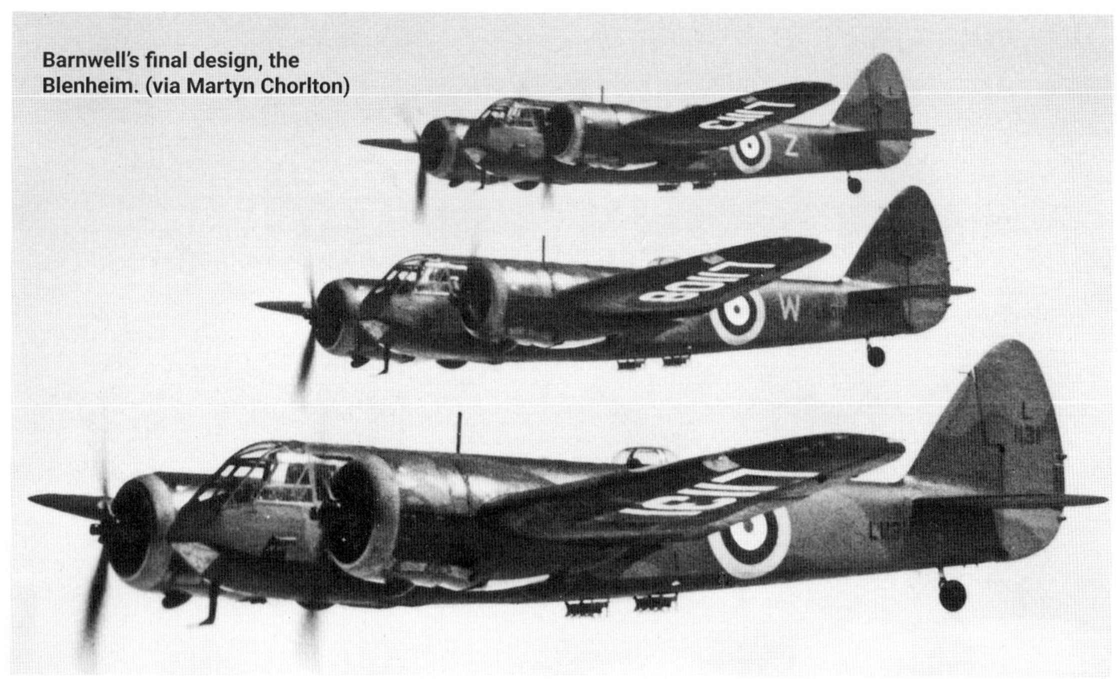

Barnwell's final design, the Blenheim. (via Martyn Chorlton)

The prototype Bristol Bulldog Mk IIA. (via Martyn Chorlton)

Chapter 7

Blitzkrieg on the Western Front

For the first few weeks of the Second World War, the Blenheims of 2 Group were on permanent readiness for a potential transfer to Northern France. Ten squadrons of Fairey Battles from 1 Group had already taken up residence across the Channel as part of the AASF (Advanced Airborne Striking Force) but, by the middle of October 1939, moves were afoot to begin converting some of them to the Blenheim Mk IV. 15 and 40 Squadrons were the first, carrying out their conversion at Wyton, the home of 114 and 139 Squadrons who had been operating the Blenheim for several years.

Prior to this, 53 Squadron were the first Blenheim Mk IV unit to arrive in France on September 20, 1939 when they moved from Odiham to Plivot. Four days later, 18 and 57 Squadrons – both flying Mk Is and Mk IVs and both from Upper Heyford – remained together in France when they moved to Roye/Amy. 59 Squadron's Mk IVs followed from Andover on October 5, settling at Poix, with detachments operating from Vitry-en-Artois and Rennes. They were joined by 53 Squadron on October 11 while 18 and 57 Squadrons remained a couple when both were repositioned to Rosières-en-Santerre on October 17/18. These four units were all under BEF (British Expeditionary Force) control.

101 Squadron Blenheim MK IV, one of many which played its part in the Battle of France operating from West Raynham, Manston and Brize Norton. (*Aeroplane*)

57 Squadron arrived in France in September 1939 with the Mk I but by March 1940 had received the Mk IV. After suffering heavy losses the unit returned to England on May 22, 1940.

114 Squadron had been operating a handful of Blenheims on detachment from late September but, on December 9, had moved *en masse* to Condé/Vraux, while 139 Squadron had moved to Bétheniville eight days earlier. Both were under AASF control.

Reconnaissance – no milk run!

All six Blenheim squadrons in the theatre were tasked with the duty of 'strategic reconnaissance' in support of all Allied Ground Forces. Until then, this had been dealt with by the Battles, which had been experiencing unsustainable losses even on reconnaissance operations (for example, on September 30 five 150 Squadron machines failed to return). Much to the relief of the Battle crews, the strategic reconnaissance was taken over by the Blenheims.

While it was true that the Battle was completely unsuited to reconnaissance operations in a 'hostile' environment, the Blenheim, while being a better aircraft to carry cameras, was no better. The press obviously highly praised the endeavours of the Blenheim crews, an example being the feature from *The Aeroplane* in this very chapter. However, from September 3 to December 31, 1939 a total of 47 reconnaissance operations were flown by Blenheims from French airfields, but only 31 of the sorties managed to take any photographs, which was of little use to the ground forces.

110 Squadron was one of the first units to receive the Mk IV, at Wattisham in June 1939. The squadron played an important role in the Battle of France and beyond. (via Martyn Chorlton)

Obviously all of these 'recce' operations had to be flown in daylight, making them a very hazardous undertaking indeed. From October 13 to November 23, nine Blenheims were lost, killing 17 aircrew, four more became PoWs and another three were interned in Belgium. The Mk Is of 57 Squadron took the brunt of these early losses in France with six aircraft lost on 'recce' sorties and two others lost in flying accidents. The first Blenheim to be lost in France also saw 57 Squadron's OC, Wg Cdr H M Day, fail to return although, unlike his two crew, he survived to become a PoW after their aircraft, L1138 was shot down near Birkenfeld in Germany.

Defensive tactics

These 'recce' forays into enemy territory quickly highlighted that the once highly praised performance of the Blenheim was distinctly lacking when faced with a determined Bf109 or Me110 attack, not to mention the flak. Early lessons learned were taken on board by 2 Group who were also flying daylight 'recce' sorties from their East Anglian bases. The poor defensive armament of the Blenheim had been a bone of contention long before the war began and, following a host of suggestions, WG Cdr B Embry's proposal of fitting a Bristol type gun turret with twin VGO 0.303in machine-guns was accepted. The VGO guns would later be replaced by Brownings and an additional

59 Squadrons Blenheims Mk IVs arrived at Poix on October 5, 1939 and remained there until May 19, 1940 when the unit briefly relocated at Crécy. By the next day, the remnants of the squadron were moved to Lympne and on to Andover. (via Martyn Chorlton)

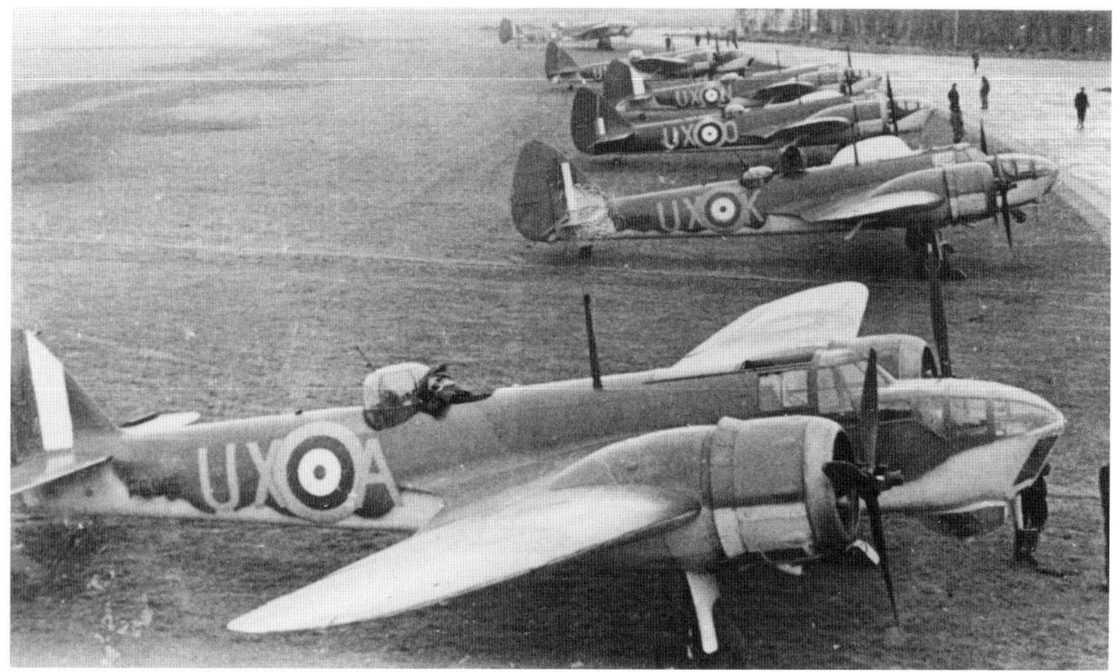

82 Squadron suffered terrible losses during the Battle of France, especially during a raid on Gembloux on May 17, 1940 when all 12 Blenheims that left Watton failed to return.

gimbal-mounted 0.303in was also fitted into the nose, operated by the observer. Self-sealing fuel tanks was another modification that was implemented but many more Blenheims would be lost before all of these updates were carried out.

The seven Blenheim squadrons that made up 2 Group by the beginning of 1940 were originally destined to be sent to France but a lack of suitable airfields put paid to this. The group was dedicated to flying anti-shipping sorties and keeping a close eye on all enemy shipping movements. These daylight operations were flown in daylight and their only form of defence was to keep as tight a formation as possible when attacked by enemy fighters. One example took place on January 10, 1940 when a formation of Blenheims, led by Sqn Ldr K Doran DFC, was bounced by five Bf110s. The story was covered in *The Aeroplane* on January 26, 1940:

"The engagement which took place between enemy fighters of the type Messerschmitt Me 110 and Bristol Blenheim bombers of the RAF in the North Sea on the 10th January, 1940, was of particular interest from a tactical point of view. The latest accounts of the incident show that the nine Blenheims were at the time on their way to carry out a reconnaissance over an area in the Eastern portion of the North Sea.

"The Blenheims were flying in formation at a height of about 6,000 feet when they were intercepted by the Messerschmitts, about 150 miles N.N.W. of Borkum. Sighting the Messerschmitts, the leader closed up his formation and turned to a North-Westerly course to draw the enemy farther from his bases. As soon as the enemy attacks developed, the leader led his formation down to sea level so as to reduce the number of directions from which the enemy could deliver attacks, and to confine them to the upper hemisphere.

"The top speed of the Messerschmitt 110 is reported to be about 365 miles an hour, which gives it a very considerable superiority over the Blenheim, and it is very heavily armed both with machine

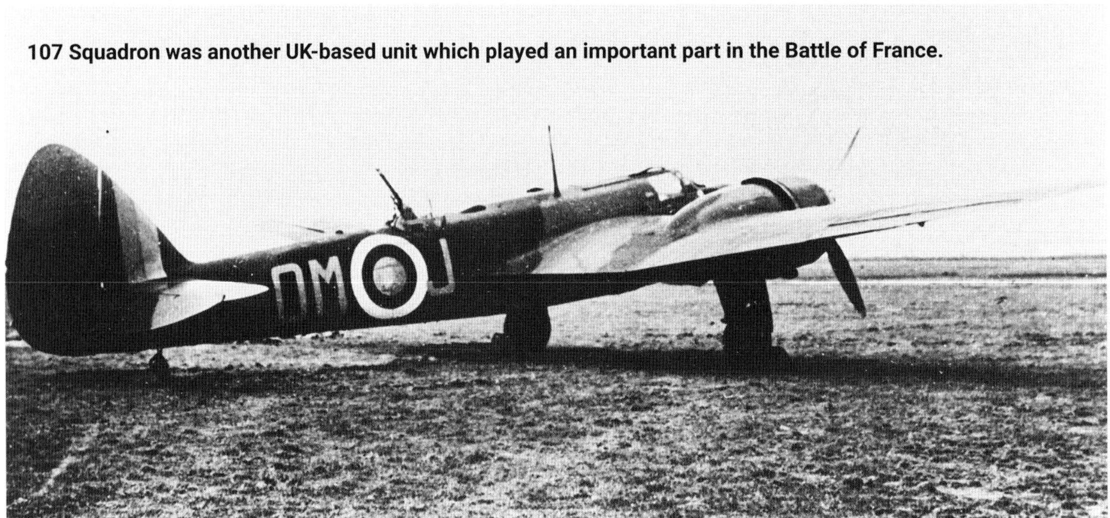

107 Squadron was another UK-based unit which played an important part in the Battle of France.

guns and cannons. Yet the Blenheims, by virtue mainly of admirable leadership and good discipline, proved themselves more than a match for Germany's most formidable fighters.

"For 20 minutes these crack fighters of the German Air Force strove to break down the cohesion of the British formation. The Messerschmitt fighters delivered their attacks with great rapidity, both from head on, from the beam, as well as from directly astern.

"In spite of every effort and of simultaneous attacks from different directions, the Messerschmitts failed to make any appreciable impression on the steadiness of the Blenheim formation.

"The only loss to the Blenheims occurred in one of the first attacks when the engine of one of our aircraft was put out of action and the aircraft was consequently compelled to fall astern where it was

Press day at Wyton in June 1940 gives no hint of the dangers that these 40 Squadron Blenheim crews were facing during operations over France.

The same press day at Wyton which also shows examples of other Battle of France participants, including 15, 82, 107 and 110 Squadrons.

immediately set on by several Messerschmitts and shot down into the sea.

"The remaining eight Blenheims immediately closed up again into even tighter formation, and soon had the satisfaction of seeing a Messerschmitt receive the full blast of their concentrated fire and throw up a great column of water as it crashed into the sea.

"This success was soon followed up by further signs of the discomfiture of the enemy. After one of the Messerschmitts had attempted a beam attack and had come under heavy fire from the Blenheims, it turned away with every appearance of having been hit and made off in a South-Easterly direction towards the German coast.

"This one was soon followed by the hasty retirement in the same direction of another of the Messerschmitts, which must certainly have been seriously damaged. Of these two it

One of the 12 Blenheims of 82 Squadron which was lost on the Gembloux raid on May 17, 1940. This is L9213, which was shot down near Presles-et-Thierney, killing the three crew instantly.

is now known that one was forced to come down in Denmark, where the crew was interned, and it is possible that the other failed to reach land and came down in the sea. After these losses the remaining enemy fighters held back and attempted no further attacks, confining themselves to following the formation at a distance in the hope, perhaps, of having a chance of a straggler later on. In this they were disappointed."

It was Blenheim Mk IV P4859, flown by Sgt J H Hanne and crew of 110 Squadron, which crashed into the sea while two others, N6203 and N6213, crash landed at Manby and Wattisham respectively, without injury to the crews. This skirmish showed, with calm leadership and concentrated defensive fire the Blenheim, on occasion, could fight back.

'Suddenly the war became bloody dangerous'

Poor weather during January and February 1940 had seen the Blenheim squadrons spend far more time on the ground than in the air. Operations, which mainly revolved around reconnaissance and training sorties, continued through March and April but by the beginning of May 1940, things began to hot up on the Continent.

The German forces were preparing to make rapid advances across the Continent and the Blenheim squadrons would have to play their part in supporting the BEF. However, even at this early stage there were doubts on how best to employ the light bomber force which undoubtedly would have proved invaluable in support of an advancing army. This scenario envisaged the Blenheims up against an advancing army which would be well supported with a variety of anti-aircraft weaponry and a strong attacking fighter force. Unfortunately, this was exactly how the Blenheim was employed during the Battle of France, operating at low level in small groups putting both aircrew and aircraft at unnecessary risk.

It was on May 10 that the German forces began their three-pronged attack on Holland, Belgium and France, leaving the Allied forces in complete disarray as its commanders struggled to work out exactly how to tackle the threat. The first RAF Blenheim sortie from France was by a 53 Squadron aircraft from Poix which took off at 0855hrs. After being damaged by light flak, Plt Off D Massey and crew managed to land at Vitry at 1140hrs where the aircraft was abandoned to its fate. In the words of one Blenheim pilot, 'Suddenly the war became bloody dangerous.'

Thirteen Blenheim squadrons were at the disposal of 2 Group and the Air Component of the BEF

Another victim of the Gembloux raid was P6893, seen here at Watton in happier days. The bomber was lost without trace.

on the day the German forces struck. Six of these were operating from France, while 15, 21, 40, 82, 101, 107 and 110 Squadrons flew from their East Anglian bases. This equated to 230 Mk IVs available, 108 of them in France.

Several airfields were bombed in France during the early hours of May 10, but generally most escaped unscathed while the Blenheim force responded in low numbers in an attempt to report on the positions of the advancing enemy troop columns. By the end of the day though, six Blenheims had been lost on hazardous reconnaissance operations, two each from 18, 57 and 40 Squadrons. The latter, operating from Wyton, also launched an attack on Ypenburg, losing three of the 12 aircraft involved in the raid. 600 Squadron had been in action from Manston since the early hours and, at 1650hrs, six Mk IFs joined a dozen Mk IVs of 110 Squadron from Wattisham on a low level bombing and strafing raid. The target was a group of Ju52s which had been seen on a beach north of Hague. On their arrival, the Blenheims were greeted with heavy anti-aircraft fire and several determined attacks by Me110s but still managed to destroy several of the transports on the ground before making their escape. All but one Blenheim made it back to England, each and every one of them with a memento of the successful attack.

May 11 saw 114 Squadron effectively removed from the battle after their airfield at Conde/Vraux was bombed, destroying six Blenheims on the ground. Only those Blenheims based in England could respond this day while the BEF licked its wounds. 110 Squadron left Wattisham at 1500hrs with a dozen Blenheims followed by eleven more from 21 Squadron from Bodney. Their target was enemy troop positions on bridges over the Maas which were heavily defended by both flak and fighters. Two 110 Squadron aircraft were lost and, once again, of those that survived, all returned with flak damage. That evening, it was the turn of 15 Squadron from Alconbury, 107 Squadron from Wattisham and 139 Squadron from Plivot to attack bridges over the Albert Kanaal at Maastricht. The raid was a total disaster with 15 Squadron losing six aircraft, 107 Squadron four and 139 Squadron seven Blenheims. Thirty-six aircrew were killed and just nine survived to become PoWs.

Above: One of many that failed to return from the massed Blenheim and Battle attacks on bridges in the Sedan area. This is L9241 of 110 Squadron which force landed near Orchies, 15 miles SSE of Lille. The crew – Sgt A R Storrow, Sgt E C Parker and LAC Rowlands – all evaded capture and made it safely back to England.

Right: Action photo taken during an attack by Blenheims on bridges over the Meuse at Maastricht in June 1940.

In the vain hope of trying to recover their strength, no Bomber Command operations were flown on May 13, but the following day, an all-out effort was flown, once again in an attempt to stop the German forces pushing through. The targets were bridges in the Sedan area and again the attacking Blenheims and even more so the Battles which were being despatched in broad daylight were easy pickings for flak and fighters. As a result, the RAF Bomber Command had achieved a casualty percentage rate which would never be exceeded for the remainder of the war. Fourteen Blenheims were lost this day – all but one during the Sedan raids – plus an alarming 33 Battles. This does not include the many aircraft which did manage to return to their home airfields but were so badly damaged that they would never fly again.

May continued to see aircrew losses mounting and, by May 22, 2 Group had lost 44 of its Blenheims, resulting in over 100 killed. By the end of May this figure had reached 150 which equated to nine squadrons of bombers. While aircraft could be replaced, the crews lost during this period were virtually all pre-war trained professionals whose experience would prove a great loss to the RAF.

From May 26, Operation Dynamo began and the remaining Blenheims continued to fight on, providing what air support they could. After nearly 340,000 troops had been evacuated, Blenheim operations continued over France, which included the now daily offensive on the advancing German forces. By the time the French surrendered on June 22, 1940, another 40 Blenheims had been lost but like all forces in a time of war, the force would re-group, re-form and fight on. The chaos and tragedy over France would be quickly forgotten as the next phase of the war, the Battle of Britain, began.

One of many Blenheims abandoned on French airfields following the evacuation of the BEF in early June 1940.

The War in The Air From *The Aeroplane,* January 26, 1940

Below will be found the 20th instalment of contemporary accounts of The War in the Air. Such summaries of the week's happenings will be continued for present information and future reference.

Reconnaissance photographs taken over Germany and now released by the Air Ministry for publication give some idea of the extent of this phase of the work of the Royal Air Force since the War began. The few photographs published have been selected from many thousands which are being increased in numbers daily.

Close examination of most of those now published reveals that they were taken months ago while the trees were still in leaf. Later photographs are still more interesting. The fact that many of them were taken from below 3,000 ft. is a comment on the inefficiency of German air defence and the way in which the fast bomber may get away unmolested.

Germany certainly has some useful photographs of this country and France as the result of reconnaissance by its bombers. But they do not approach the numbers of those obtained over enemy territory by the RAF and the Armee de l'Air.

Bristol Blenheims have repeatedly taken off before dawn from their stations in England, flown out to sea and into Germany North of the Netherlands frontiers. They have flown down the whole length of the Siegfried Line, often low down, and, after exposing all their plates, have landed in France. Next day, they have made the return trip in the opposite direction.

A glimpse of the high spirit of these crews of the Bomber Command is given by one incident when the pilot of a Blenheim saw two German aeroplanes landing at one aerodrome over which he was passing. He paused to dive on them and shoot them up before resuming his photographic beat.

As well as photographing the land defences of the enemy and their aerodromes up to areas far behind the lines, the Royal Air Force has photographed all the harbours and estuaries up the German coast from Holland to Denmark.

Just as we have stopped using Battles for photographic reconnaissance – a job for which they were not designed – so the Germans appear to have stopped sending Dornier Do 17s on similar errands over our lines. The losses to the Do 17s were becoming very heavy, in spite of high flying tactics. The big Heinkel He 111Ks are now being used are more difficult to catch and kill, but, even so, have been shot down in fair numbers. Curiously enough, these Heinkels seem to be more difficult to disable than they were when the War began and there is reason to believe that the crews are now provided with some measure of armour plate around their positions. The 'bullet-proof' fuel tanks appear to be surprisingly efficient and the Heinkels can 'carry a lot of lead' without being completely disabled. These facts seem to demand the adoption of cannon in our fighters. One hit from a cannon-shell is almost certain to bring down an enemy aeroplane wherever it may hit.

That leads also to the subject of the amount of ammunition desirable to be carried by a fighter. As bombers become better defended against attack more fire is needed to destroy them. On several occasions recently fighters on both sides have had to break off combat with bombers because they have exhausted all their ammunition. Yet the tendency is to put more and more guns into a fighter.

Thus, with the demand for more guns and more ammunition for each of them, the size of the fighter must increase. Eventually, when we come to the fighter armed not with multi machine-guns but with multi-cannons and a plentiful supply of shells for them, the machine will have to be much bigger than anything normally thought of as a fighter at present.

This question of ammunition is a reason for the lack of escorting in the War so far — except the escorting of our bombers into and out of Heligoland and Wilhelmshaven for some hundreds of miles by Messerschmitt Me 110s. Escort fighters which use all their ammunition in one scrap are then useless to help their formation any more. Another point, in these days of high speeds, is that to turn away from a bomber formation to engage assailants is often to lose it.

This War is slowly revealing many points of aerial tactics never fully realised before.

Chapter 8

The Operational Training Units

'Survive OTU and you will survive the war'

The RAF's OTUs were the crucial final stage before fledgling aircrew were posted to an operational squadron. Unfortunately, despite many months of training, far too many young airmen lost their lives during this final stage. 55,500 airmen lost their lives serving with Bomber Command during the Second World War. However, twice as many again were killed during training and this is not widely recognised. The statement 'Survive OTU and you will survive the war' became a disturbing reality.

When the first Blenheim OTUs were formed in April 1940 there was still a demand for new Blenheims (by this time purely Mk IVs) to be supplied directly to the operational squadrons. OTUs would have to make do with discarded Mk Is, many of which had already seen a great deal of use with a squadron but, at this stage of the war, had at least not been in action. By late 1940, this situation changed as the Mk IV began to be supplied to the second-line OTUs as well, giving those units specifically designed to re-supply 2 Group – such as 13 and 17 OTU – the opportunity to train its new crews on the same aircraft they would take into action.

The Blenheim (and not just Mk IF and Mk IVF variants) also found a very useful secondary role for training night fighter crews, even though the Beaufighter was rapidly being introduced into service to take over this role. 54 OTU in particular at Charterhall (with an unenviable loss rate which saw the airfield renamed as 'slaughter hall'), operated its Blenheims in the night fighter training role until 1944. Admittedly by this time the only significant mark still be operated was the Mk V, many of which never reached operational squadrons and were sent direct to OTUs.

At least 1,200 Blenheims of all marks served with 30 OTUs in Britain, Canada, the Middle East and the Far East from 1940 through to 1945. At least a third of these served with more than one OTU as well, giving thousands of young bomber crews their first taste of performing as an operational crew.

Mk IV V6083 of 13 OTU from Bicester, presents us with a nice view of the rearward firing chin turret and the dorsal turret fitted with a pair of machine guns rather than the ineffective single VGO gun. Flame-damped exhausts and fuel jettison pipes are also visible. (*Aeroplane*)

The OTUs

(detailing RAF and RCAF Blenheim/Bolingbroke locations, movements and establishments only)

1 (Coastal) OTU

Formed April 1, 1940 ex-Coastal Command Landplane Pilots Pool within 17 Group based at Silloth, Cumbria. At first, courses were run on the Anson, Blenheim, Beaufort and Hudson pending the formation of 2, 3 and 5 OTUs. 'D' Flight operated eight Blenheims in a supporting role and from August 9 to November 11, 1940 was detached to Prestwick. Not long after returning to Silloth, all Blenheims on strength were transferred to 2 OTU.

Establishment
24 aircraft used by the unit in total, of which eight were Blenheims (Mk I and Mk IV).

2 (Coastal) OTU

Formed October 1, 1940 in 17 Group at Catfoss, East Yorkshire to train twin-engined strike crews, at first using Blenheims and Ansons. Ex-'D' Flight of 1 OTU continued its detachment at Prestwick under 2 OTU control until July 1941. From June 1941 the Beaufighter began to arrive but the Blenheim remained the principle type until early 1942. 2 OTU Blenheims were also detached to Driffield (Oct 40 to early 1941), Sherburn-in-Elmet and Hutton Cranswick (Feb 1942).

Establishment
May 1941; nine Blenheim (dual) and 22 Mk IV. Feb 1942; 16 Mk IV, 32 Blenheim/Beaufighter and 24 Mk Is. Operated 114 Blenheims from Oct 1940 to early 1942.
Aircraft Mk I, Mk IV and Mk V.

3 (Coastal) OTU

Formed November 27, 1940 in 17 Group at Chivenor, Devon taking over the responsibility of training Anson and Beaufort crews from 1 OTU. Presuming the Blenheim played a supporting role with the OTU from late 1940 through 1941. **Establishment** *19 Blenheims used by the unit in total.*
Aircraft *Mk I and Mk IV.*

5 OTU

Formed March 15, 1940 at Aston Down, Gloucestershire to train fighter pilots on a variety of types, including the Blenheim Mk IF. Redesignated 55 OTU on November 1, 1940 and all Blenheims and Defiants on strength were transferred to 54 OTU.

Establishment
Mar 1940; 12 Mk IF.
Oct 1940; 24 Mk IF
30 Blenheims used by the unit in total.
Aircraft Mk IF.

5 (Coastal) OTU

Unit reformed at Chivenor in 17 Group on August 1, 1941 to train Beaufort and Hampden crews in the torpedo role. Blenheims played a supporting role during 1941 and 1942.

Establishment
17 Blenheims used by the unit in total.
Aircraft Mk IV.

6 (Coastal) OTU

Reformed on June 1, 1942 from 2 School of Army Co-Operation at Andover, Hampshire within 17 Group, operating the Blenheim. Disbanded into 42 OTU on July 18, 1941. Unit reformed at Thornaby, North Yorkshire on July 19, 1941 within 17 Group. A few Blenheim MK IVs were flown in a supporting role.

Establishment
Approximately 50 Blenheims (mainly Mk Is passed through the original 6[C]OTU.
Aircraft Mk I and Mk IV.

12 OTU

Formed April 8, 1940 from 1 Group Pool (52 and 53 Squadrons) at Benson, Oxfordshire to train light bomber crews. Only operated three Blenheims in a supporting role in 1940.
Establishment Three Mk Is.
Aircraft Mk I.

13 OTU

Formed on April 8, 1940 at Bicester, Oxfordshire from 2 Group Pool (104 and 108 Squadrons) for training Blenheim light day bomber crews. Night intruder training was also later introduced later. Unit also made use of RLGs at Weston-on-the-Green (Apr 8 to Nov 1, 40), Hinton-in-the-Hedges (Nov 1, 40 to Aug 23, 42), Finmere (Jul 31, 42 to Jul 27, 45) and Turweston

A familiar sight in East Yorkshire from late 1940 through to 1942 were the Blenheims of 2 OTU. This happy crew was photographed at Catfoss in early 1941. (via Martyn Chorlton)

(Oct 1, 42 to Nov 28, 42 and May 1 to Jul 3, 43). Jul 15, 1940 unit transferred to 7 Group, which became 92 Group on May 11, 1942. Mitchells, Bostons and some Mosquitoes (temporarily) began to arrive from May 1943 but a strong Blenheim presence remained. Transferred to 70 Group June 1943 and then to 9 Group on November 1, 1943. Mosquitoes reintroduced in numbers and the remaining Blenheims left the unit in April 1944.

Establishment
Apr 1940; 18 Blenheims.
May 1940; 32 Mk IV, 16 Mk I (dual)
Aug 1941; 48 Blenheim
May 1943; 29 Blenheim
265 Blenheims passed through 13 OTU from April 1940 to April 1944.
Aircraft *Mk I, Mk IV and Mk V.*

15 OTU

Formed April 8, 1940 from 3 Group Pool (75 and 148 Squadrons) at Harwell, Oxfordshire to train night bomber crews. A few Blenheims were operated in a supporting role in 1940.
Establishment *Four Mk Is.*
Aircraft *Mk I.*

17 OTU

Formed April 8, 1940 from 6 Group at Upwood, Cambridgeshire to train light bomber crews on the Blenheim. Operated a detachment from Squires Gate (April 8 to June 40). Also had the luxury of three satellite airfields at Warboys (May 17, 41 to Aug 5, 42), Steeple Morden (Jan 14 to May 4, 43) and Polebrook (Jan 16 to Jun 41). June 16, 1940 unit transferred to 7 Group and on Dec 15, 1941 the operational and synthetic flights were moved to Warboys. May 5, 1942 unit transferred to 92 Group. From June 1942 the amount of Blenheims on

As the war progressed a large number Blenheim Mk IVs found themselves being delivered direct to second-line units; V5382 was a good example. After carrying out trials work with the A&AEE the bomber was transferred to 2 SAC, 6, 42 and 51 OTUs. It was serving with the latter that its career came to an end at Cranfield on September 24, 1942.

strength was reduced and prior to the unit moving to Silverstone, Northamptonshire none remained.
Establishment
May 1940; 32 Mk IV, 16 Mk I (dual).
Aug 1941; 48 Blenheim
Jun 1942; 48 Blenheim
Sep 1942; seven Mk I
184 Blenheims saw service with 17 OTU from April 1940 to the spring of 1942.
Aircraft *Mk I and Mk IV.*

18 OTU

Formed June 15, 1940 from the Polish Training Unit in 6 Group at Hucknall, Nottinghamshire to train light bomber for Polish Battle squadrons. A handful of Blenheim Mk Is were operated in a supporting role.
Establishment *Unknown.*
Aircraft *Mk I.*

31 OTU

Formed May 23, 1941 at Derbert, Nova Scotia, Canada in 3 Training Command to train GR crews on the Hudson. Operated a few Bolingbrokes in a supporting role before disbanding into 7 OTU, RCAF on July 1, 1944.

Establishment *Unknown.*
Aircraft *Bolingbroke Mk I and IV-T.*

34 OTU

Formed in Britain and them embarked at Gourock in the *Batory* on April 8, 1942. Arrived Yarmouth, Nova Scotia, Canada on April 17, 1942 to form a GR unit within 3 Training Command. Moved to Pennfield Ridge, New Brunswick in May 1942, later disbanding there on May 19, 1944. Operated the Bolingbroke in a supporting role.
Establishment *Unknown.*
Aircraft *Bolingbroke Mk IV-T.*

36 OTU

Formed in Britain and then embarked for Canada in the HMT *Orbita* on February 24, 1942. Arrived Greenwood, Nova Scotia in March 1942 to train GR crews in 3 Training Command. Disbanded and replaced by 8 OTU, RCAF on June 30, 1944. Once again the Bolingbroke was operated in a supporting role.
Establishment *Unknown.*
Aircraft *Bolingbroke Mk IV-T.*

42 OTU

Formed July 18, 1941 in 70 Group, Army Co-Operation Command at Andover to train crews for army support duties. Part of the instructional staff was from 6OTU to help train the many Lysander pilots to fly the Blenheim in anticipation of the influx of ground-support Bisleys which were planned to enter service. With the introduction of the Mk V light bomber instead, the requirement for this type of training declined. A satellite at Thruxton was used from July 1941 to October 10, 1942. Two weeks later the unit moved to Ashbourne and in May 1943 42 OTUs role changed to that of training crews for glider towing squadrons. With little requirement for the Blenheim for this task, the type entered a decline and on July 11, 1943 the last one left 42 OTU.

Establishment

Jan 1942; 24 Mk V, 12 Mk I.
121 Blenheims served with 42 OTU from July 1941 to July 1943.
Aircraft Mk I and Mk V.

51 OTU

Formed July 26, 1941 in 81 Group at Debden, Essex to train night fighter crews with Blenheims and a handful of Havocs for Turbinlite training. Moved to Cranfield, Bedfordshire on August 17, 1941 with a satellite at Twinwood Farm (Aug 17, 41 to Jun 14, 45). The Beaufighter and later the Mosquito went on to become the major types on strength although the last Blenheim was not phased out until early 1945.

Establishment

Aug 1941; 52 Mk I, Mk IV and Mk VB or Havoc, eight Mk I, MK IV or Hudson.
Jul 1942; 13 Blenheim AI, 14 Blenheim (solo'), 12 Blenheim (dual)

Several Blenheim Mk Vs saw service with UK-based OTUs, with many of them serving well into 1944. (via Martyn Chorlton)

Jul 1943; ten Mk V (dual), four Mk I and Mk IV
Dec 1944; one Mk V
101 Blenheims served 51 OTU from July 1941 to early 1945.
Aircraft Mk I, Mk IV and Mk V.

52 OTU

Formed March 3, 1941 in 81 Group at Debden, Essex with Hurricanes to train fighter pilots. Moved to Aston Down on August 8, 1941 by which time it is not known if any Blenheims were still operating in a supporting role.

Establishment Mar 1941; one Mk I.
Aircraft Mk I and Mk V.

54 OTU

Formed on November 25, 1940 in 12 Group at Church Fenton, North Yorkshire to train night fighter crews. From June 1941, all single-engined types, mainly Defiants were transferred to 60 OTU and 54 OTU became a twin-engined training unit. From February 1942 Beaufighters began to replace the Blenheim but on moving to Charterhall in May 1942 many remained on strength. The Blenheim was phased out by early 1944.

Establishment

Nov 1940; 23 Blenheims, eight Mk I (dual).
Aug 1941; 52 Mk I, Mk IV and Mk Vs or Beaufighter Mk II, eight Mk I, Mk V or Hudson.
Jul 1942; 13 Blenheim AI, 12 Blenheim (dual), 14 Blenheim (solo).
Jan 1944; two Mk V.
176 Blenheims passed through 54 OTU from November 1940 to early 1944.
Aircraft Mk I, Mk IV and Mk V.

55 OTU

Formed on November 11, 1940 in 10 Group at Aston Down, from 5 OTU as a fighter training unit with Hurricanes, Blenheims, Defiants and Masters. A detachment was formed at Moreton-on-Marsh from November 27, 1940 to February 22, 1941 but by the end of 1940 both the Blenheim and Defiant flights had been transferred to 54 OTU.

Establishment Nov 1940; seven Mk I.
Aircraft Mk I.

56 OTU

Formed November 11, 1940 in 81 Group at Sutton Bridge, Lincolnshire to train fighter pilots on Hurricanes. A couple of Blenheims are credited to have served with this unit, most likely from late 1940 to late 1941.

Establishment Nov 1940; two Mk I.
Aircraft Mk I.

60 OTU

Formed April 28, 1941 in 81 Group at Leconfield, North Yorkshire to train night fighter crews on the Blenheim and Defiant. On June 4, 1941 the unit was moved to East Fortune, East Lothian becoming a dedicated Defiant OTU. By October 1941 the unit was converted to a twin-engined night fighter training unit which saw an influx of Beaufighters and Blenheims for the task. 60 OTU was disbanded on November 24, 1942 and redesignated as 132 OTU the same day, now operating under 17 Group control, Coastal Command, still at East Fortune.

60 OTU was reformed on May 17, 1943 in 9 Group at High Ercall, Shropshire to train intruder crews on the Mosquito. By the summer only a handful of Blenheims were operating in a supporting role.

Establishment
Oct 1941; 52 Blenheim (18 with AI), eight Blenheim (dual).
Jul 1942; 13 Blenheim AI, 12 Blenheim (dual), 14 Blenheim (solo).
Jul 1943; two Mk V.
109 Blenheims served through both of 60 OTUs guises from April 1941 to mid-1943.
Aircraft Mk I, Mk IV and Mk V.

63 OTU

Formed September 7, 1943 in 9 Group at Honiley, Warwickshire to train night fighter crews on the Beaufighter. A pair of Mk V (dual) served through to the summer of 1944.

Establishment
Sep 1943; two Mk V (dual)
Feb 1944; two Mk V (dual)
Aircraft Mk V.

70 (Middle East) OTU

Formed December 12, 1940 at Ismailia, Egypt from the Training Unit and Reserve Pool to train pilots in the conditions likely to be encountered during their tours of duty in the Middle East. 'A' Flight operated Blenheims at first with a detachment operating from Nakuru, Kenya from March 30 to July 28, 1941. From April 1941 the unit concentrated on training light and medium bomber crews and also AI operators.

In July 1941 the unit moved as a whole to Nakuru to operate directly under Training Command, Middle East. Not long after 70 OTU began a short conversion course from the Oxford to the Blenheim, the first training 53 SAAF pilots. Blenheims remained on strength until August 1943 when while at Shandur the type was superseded by the Marauder.

Establishment
Dates unknown but 141 Blenheims served with 70 OTU during its existence.
Aircraft Mk I, Mk IV and Mk V.

71 OTU

Formed June 1, 1941 in 202 Group at Ismailia to take over 70 OTUs fighter training element. Moved to Gordon's Tree in September 1941 and again to Carthago, Tunisia in May 1942. Returning to Ismailia in May 1943, 71 OTU was disbanded in June 1945. During this period a handful of Blenheims flew a supporting role.

Establishment
Dates unknown but at least two Blenheims were operated by the unit.
Aircraft Mk IV and Mk V.

72 OTU

Formed November 10, 1941 at Carthago but moved to Wadi Gazouza eight days later absorbing a nucleus left by 211 Squadron. The unit was to train light bomber crews under tropical conditions with Blenheims, Bostons and Ansons. Main party left for

The Blenheim Mk V was a more familiar sight throughout the Middle East compared to the European theatre. This Mk V served with an OTU through to early 1945. (*Aeroplane*)

Nanyuki, Kenya by sea on March 20, 1942 arriving 13 days later. Under 207 Group control, the unit saw its days out under AHQ East Africa until May 14, 1943.

Establishment

Apr 1942; 72 Blenheims
85 different Blenheims served with this unit from late 1941 to May 1943.
Aircraft *Mk I, Mk IV and Mk V.*

73 OTU

Formed January 1, 1942 in 207 Group at Sheikh Othman, Aden to train fighter pilots under desert conditions. At least one Blenheim served with the unit during 1942.

Establishment *1942; one Mk I*
Aircraft *Mk I.*

Women flight line mechanics were a common sight in the RAF from 1941 onwards, especially at OTUs. (via Martyn Chorlton)

75 OTU

Formed December 8, 1942 at Gianaclis, Egypt to train GR crews under local conditions. From January 1943 absorbed 1 METS and the Twin-Engine Conversion and Refresher Flight and by May the unit was under 203 Group control. Moved to Shallufa in February 1945 and was disbanded by June.

Establishment

Feb 1943; 12 Blenheims.
Mar 1943; 17 Blenheims.
At least 28 Blenheims passed through 75 OTU well into 1944.
Aircraft *Mk I, Mk IV and Mk V.*

79 OTU

Formed February 1, 1944 at Nicosia, Cyprus to train GR and strike crews although aircraft did not arrive until April. From May flying training began making use of satellites at Tymbou (Sep 27, 44 to Jul 30, 45) and Lakatamia (Oct 1 to Dec 19, 44 and Jan to 7 Jul 45). Blenheims served right through to the disbandment of 79 OTU on July 30, 1945.

Establishment

May 1945; 16 Mk V. 31 Blenheims served with 79OTU throughout its short career.
Aircraft *Mk V.*

132 (Coastal) OTU

Formed November 24, 1942 in 17 Group at East Fortune from 60 OTU to train long-range fighter and strike crews for Coastal Command squadrons. Initial equipment was the Blenheim and Beaufighter but by the summer of 1943, the former had been replaced by the Beaufort.

Establishment

Dec 1942; 13 Mk I (AI), Mk I and Mk V (dual), 14 Mk I, Mk IV and Mk V.
72 Blenheims served 132 OTU, many of them having already served with 60 OTU.
Aircraft *Mk I, IV and Mk V.*

152 (Bomber) OTU

Formed October 22, 1942 in 227 Group at Peshawar to train pilots from FTSs in India. All marks of Blenheim were operated until the unit was disbanded in March 1944.

Establishment *Seven Blenheims*
Aircraft *Mk I, Mk IV and Mk V.*

The belly pack seen in this head on view gives away this aircraft as a Mk IF belonging to a night fighter training OTU. (via Martyn Chorlton)

Chapter 9

Night Owls

Air cover against possible night bombing raids was spread thinly in the Midland region at the beginning of 1940. Night fighter squadrons in that part of the country came under the control of 12 Group of Fighter Command whose patch stretched across the heartland of England from The Wash to the Mersey and from York to Birmingham.

Equipped with the Blenheim Mk I, 23 Squadron moved to Wittering from Northolt in May 1938 and thence to Collyweston, Wittering's adjacent satellite field, from where, at the end of March 1940, it began defensive night patrols. Initially, five Blenheims were converted to the Mk IF version by the addition of a bolt-on under-belly tray containing four .303in machine guns. This was in addition to a single forward-firing .303in machine gun fitted as standard in the wing root, plus the dorsal turret gun.

Right from the onset of war, a small number of 23 Squadron's Blenheims – first one, then later two sections at a time – were detached to Digby for a week in rotation, carrying out night readiness duty, standing patrols and searchlight co-operation sorties in that sector but with little to show for their effort.

23 Squadron in combat

The night of June 18/19, 1940, however, was crystal clear when the Luftwaffe mounted its first large scale night raid of the war on mainland British targets with over 70 aircraft. From its base at Collyweston, 23 Squadron was in action that night, deploying seven Blenheim Mk IFs on night fighter patrols in the vicinity of The Wash. The RAF was involved from the Thames to the Humber on this particular night in the form of 23, 29 and 604 Squadrons with Blenheims and 19, 66 and 74 Squadrons with Spitfires. The overall Luftwaffe raiding force was composed of Gruppen from KG.4 and KG.27 for whom places such as Mildenhall, Honington and Marham were the primary objectives.

Sqn Ldr Joseph 'Spike' O'Brien in L8687, 'X' was first up from Collyweston at 2230hrs. Seated at his shoulder in the navigator's position was Plt Off Cuthbert King-Clarke, a new pilot being shown the

23 Sqn Blenheim Mk IF YP-Q at Wittering, January 1940

ropes by his CO. Back in the turret was air-gunner Cpl David Little. Six other Blenheims of 'A' and 'B' Flights left for their patrol lines at ten minute intervals. Sgt Alan Close, pilot, with his gunner, LAC Laurence Karasek in L1458, 'S' went off at 2335hrs, followed by Plt Off Aberconway Pattinson and air-gunner Cpl William McAdam, in 'U'. Next up was Flt Lt Raymond Duke-Woolley in 'L' with AC2 Derek Bell in the turret. Plt Off Derek Willans, Flt Lt Roland Knight and Fg Off Nelson Harding flew the remaining Blenheims.

Patrol lines were taken up on bearings fanning out eastwards from Wittering and it was Sgt Close who made the first interception near King's Lynn. Searchlights in The Wash belt picked out some of the raiders and initially this helped the Blenheim crews.

There, caught in the beam of one searchlight was a Heinkel He111. Close and Karasek exchanged gunfire with the enemy aircraft but the Blenheim lacked both the speed and the firepower to kill at a relatively safe distance. Their Blenheim too was lit up in the searchlight glare and it was the enemy gunners who got the better of this exchange. A burst of gunfire from the Heinkel shattered the cockpit, probably wounding or even killing Sgt Close because the aircraft immediately dived out of control and crashed into Chapel Road, Terrington St Clement. LAC Karasek was fortunate indeed to bale out and landed safely nearby.

Map showing RAF Sectors in the Midlands in 1940. (Alistair Goodrum)

23 Squadron, Digby, July 1940. Seated from left: Ensor; Baker; Harding; Duke-Woolley; Sqn Ldr Bicknell; Sqn Ldr O'Brien; Knight; Anderson; Cooper-Key; Gawith. Standing from left: Swan; Young; Sgt Bicknell; Willans; Atkinson; Grogan; Duff; Hoole; Orgias; Pushman; Gillespie; Burton; Penford; Dann; Rose. (23 Squadron Association)

Riddled by gunfire in the air battle of June 18/19, 1940, Heinkel He111, 5J+DM, the bomber flown by Oblt Jordan with KG4 Gruppenkommandeur Maj von Massenbach on board, wallows like a stranded whale in The Hood shallows off Blakeney Creek. (Peter Brooks collection)

First blood to the Luftwaffe – but not for long. Flt Lt Duke-Woolley's patrol line took him towards Sutton Bridge from where he, too, saw this searchlight activity and spotted the two aircraft involved. He gave chase at full throttle and his combat report takes up the story:

"Time 0045hrs. Observed a ball of fire, which I took to be a Blenheim fighter in flames, breaking away from behind the tail of the E/A. I climbed to engage this E/A and attacked from below the tail after the searchlights were extinguished. I closed to a range of 50 yards and opened fire. E/A returned fire and appeared to throttle back suddenly. My own speed was 130–140mph and I estimate the E/A slowed to 110mph. I delivered five attacks with front guns and during these my air gunner fired seven bursts at various ranges. After the last front gun attack my air gunner reported that the E/A's port engine was on fire. As my starboard engine was now u/s, I broke off the engagement and returned to base, where several bullet holes were found in the wings and fuselage, including cannon strikes in the starboard wing and rear fuselage."

Airspeeds mentioned here may seem quite slow but certainly, in the era of the Blenheim and Defiant, night combats rarely involved speeds above 200mph.

Raymond Myles Duke-Woolley, who shot down He111 5J+DM on June 18/19, 1940. Here, as a Wg Cdr, he is just back from his fourth sortie on the day of the Dieppe raid. (Robin Duke-Woolley)

Oblt Joachim von Arnim (third left) and his crew, Fw Karl Hauck (left), Fw Wilhelm Maier (second left), Uffz Paul Gersch (right), in front of Heinkel He111, 5J+AM before the sortie on 18/19 June, 1940. (Winston Ramsey & After The Battle Publications)

Duke-Woolley claimed the E/A as a probable but his He111 H-4 had crash-landed in the shallows of Blakeney Creek on the north Norfolk coast. As the Gruppenkommandeur of II/KG.4, Mjr Dietrich Freiherr von Massenbach, his lead pilot Oberleutnant Ulrich Jordan and radio operator Ofw Max Leimer from 5J+DM waded ashore into captivity, carrying their wounded flight engineer, Fw Karl Amberger, they would have plenty of time now to wonder where their planning went wrong.

Planning the raid. Oblt Joachim von Arnim, (second left) and Oblt Ulrich Jordan (right) going over final details before the raid by KG4 on 18/19 June, 1940. (Goss/Rauchbach archive)

Sqn Ldr O'Brien's own search line took him south from Wittering where, at about 0125hrs, searchlights coned another He111 which he intercepted at 12,000ft, ten miles from Newmarket. O'Brien reported:

"Opened fire at E/A with rear [turret] gun from below and in front as it was held by searchlights. The E/A turned to port and dived. I gave him several long bursts with the front guns from 500 to 100 yards range and saw clouds of smoke from the target's starboard engine and a lesser amount from the port engine. I overshot the E/A and passed very close below and in front of him. My rear gunner put a burst into the cockpit at close range and the E/A disappeared in a diving turn apparently out of control. I suddenly lost control of my own aircraft, which spun violently to the left. Failing to recover from the spin I ordered my crew to abandon the aircraft and I followed the navigator out of the hatch."

Luftwaffe officers of KG4 as PoWs in Canada. Oblt Jordan, front second left; Maj von Massenbach, front centre; Oblt von Arnim, back third left; Lt Backhaus, back far left; Lt Simon, back centre, were all shot down in the night battle of June 18/19, 1940. (Goss/Rauchbach archive)

The latter comment is quite an understatement! One of the myths at that time was that no pilot ever got out of a spinning Blenheim alive because the only way out was through the top sliding hatch and you might fall through one or other of the airscrews! Duke-Woolley learned that Spike helped get the new boy out; undoing his seat belt and oxygen and pushing him out of the top hatch while holding his parachute ripcord. Spike said afterwards that he felt sick when the lad fell through the airscrew. The CO then had to get out himself. Grasping the wireless aerial behind the hatch, he pulled himself up by it and turned round so that his feet were on the side of the fuselage. He kicked outwards as hard as he could and felt what he thought was the tip of an airscrew blade tap him on his helmet earpiece – but luck was with him that night!

His Blenheim crashed and exploded, scattering wreckage over a wide area at Warren Hill, Newmarket. Sadly his air gunner, Cpl Little, perished. The He111P of KG.4, 5J+AM, crashed at Fleam Dyke near Six Mile Bottom.

Airborne Interception

Early in 1940, the eminent scientist Dr E G 'Taffy' Bowen CBE FRS worked not only on the development and construction of the first practical airborne radar sets – generally referred to as Airborne Interception and abbreviated to AI – but also, due to his direct involvement over several years giving him a unique position, on the elementary theory of air interception tactics. His analysis showed that first: "…a pursuing night fighter must have a speed advantage over its target. If the

Pre-war line of 29 Squadron Blenheim Mk IFs at Debden. (via Martyn Chorlton)

fighter were no faster than the target it would never catch it… if it went too fast it would overshoot. The optimum overtaking speed was about 20 to 25% greater than the aircraft being chased". Second: "In order to have a reasonable chance of completing an interception, the night fighter must be placed within a cone of about 40 or 50° behind the raider and heading on a track not more than 30° different from the target. This presented a formidable task to the ground control as it existed at that time and was not solved until the appearance of special GCI equipment towards the end of 1940."

While in approximate terms the maximum speed of a Blenheim was said to be as good as or better than its opponents - with the exception of the Junkers Ju88 – in reality, it had neither the sort of speed margin nor the weight of firepower to deal with its opponents with ease. So the Blenheim was often at a disadvantage. During those early days, few airborne radar sets were available to install in Blenheims and it was not until late July 1940 that the first AI-assisted kill was achieved in the south of England. It was a slow old business though, with only eight enemy aircraft being claimed as shot down by AI-assisted Blenheims between August and November 1940.

29 Squadron in action

Moving from Debden to Digby on June 27, 1940, 29 Squadron began its contribution to the night defence of the Midlands, also equipped with Blenheim Mk IF fighters. A few weeks later, with Sqn Ldr Charles Widdows in command, it commenced operations from Digby's satellite airfield at Wellingore.

Non-AI operational night patrols, along various predetermined compass bearings radiating from the airfield, began immediately. These were interspersed with practice flights to get used to the new AI equipment, usually referred to at this stage as RDF trials. Towards the end of July, the squadron detached two aircraft to Ternhill every evening to lend weight to the air defence of Merseyside. At this time Digby's sector ran across the width of England with Ternhill at its north-western corner.

Patrols from Ternhill were actually controlled from Digby sector ops room and, upon completion, the Blenheims either landed back at Ternhill if they were on duty the next night or made their way back to Wellingore if they were to be relieved. There was little success from these sorties but the most significant fact was that many of the Blenheims sent on these detachments were equipped with early production AI Mk III sets.

Blenheim Mk IF 'YB-L' taxying at Debden just prior to the beginning of the Second World War. (via Martyn Chorlton)

By the end of August 1940, the squadron had nine Blenheims on charge (L1290; L1292; L1324; L1330; L1472; L6637; L7135; L7153 and L8661) equipped with 'special equipment' (AI Mk III) sets and their crews were practising hard to achieve night operational status. Among them was a certain Plt Off John Randall Daniel 'Bob' Braham who, on August 17, carried out his first 'RDF' trial – an uneventful 2½-hour patrol off the Lincolnshire coast. Braham had been with the squadron since December 1938 and was destined to become the RAF's top-scoring night-fighter ace and one of its most highly decorated airmen. Braham recalls the early days of night fighting, "[Initially] We had no airborne radar and there was then only the most primitive form of ground control. Our night patrols consisted chiefly of flying over groups of flares set out in various patterns on the ground. Flares were laid out in a particular pattern and repeated every few miles over a distance of 20 to 30 miles to form a visible patrol line. From these lines we could be directed to some point in space in an attempt to intercept the enemy. It was a hit and miss affair, dependent on there being little or no cloud so that the fighter crew could see the flares from 10,000ft or more. At other times we worked with the searchlights."

First confirmed kill

29 Squadron's first confirmed 'kill' went to Plt Off Richard Rhodes and air-gunner Sgt William Gregory in L6741, a non-AI Blenheim, while detached to Ternhill. Taking off at 0132hrs on August 18 to patrol what was called the 'Mersey Blue Line', Rhodes was vectored on to a bandit and, at 0228hrs, 15 miles south-west of Chester, he spotted what appeared to be a light on the rear part of the fuselage of an aircraft. Flying towards the target, he identified it as a Heinkel but it took him no less than two hours of chasing before he could bring his Blenheim into range. By this time, having flown south at first, the enemy aircraft turned east and was making for the Lincolnshire coast but Rhodes stuck doggedly to his quarry and finally came within firing range about 25 miles off Spurn Point. He was in no frame of mind to let the enemy off the hook after such a long chase and opened fire at 400yds, expending all the ammunition in his five front guns. Now this would normally be regarded as a pretty optimistic range but his fire on this occasion was sufficient to slow down the enemy aircraft and it began to circle and lose height. Seizing the initiative, Rhodes brought the Blenheim up on its starboard side to allow his gunner to bring the turret's Vickers K machine gun to bear and Sgt Gregory promptly emptied a whole drum of 97 .303in rounds into the enemy. The target continued to lose altitude until eventually Gregory saw

29 Squadron commanding officer at Digby at the time of the night engagements in the article in 1940, was Sqn Ldr Charles Widdows.

Bob Braham on right and Bill 'Sticks' Gregory in front of a Mosquito. This distinguished and highly successful nightfighter crew learned their trade patrolling The Wash area with 29 Squadron based at Digby. (Wg Cdr Gregory)

it settle gently on the sea about ten miles west of Cromer Knoll. Sgt Bill 'Sticks' Gregory later re-trained as a Radio/Observer and subsequently teamed up with Bob Braham to forge one of the most successful night fighter crews in the RAF.

Braham opened his own score on the night of 24/25 August 1940. With Sgt Wilsden as air gunner, the pair left Wellingore at 2320hrs in non-AI, L1463 to patrol the Digby Yellow Line. After a couple of hours, control vectored Braham towards the Humber and at 8,000ft in good visibility he saw what he thought was a Heinkel or Dornier caught in a searchlight beam. Despite the bomber twisting and turning to escape the glare, Braham came in behind it and fired four long bursts from the front guns at 500 down to 100yds while Wilsden got in two good bursts from his turret gun at close range. With smoke and sparks issuing from it the enemy aircraft lost height. Braham and Wilsden didn't see the bomber crash, but Humber searchlight units reported seeing an aircraft on fire coming down in the sea immediately after the combat. While the squadron diarist confidently recorded that it: "…confirms that Plt Off Braham destroyed the enemy aircraft…", his combat report claim for a 'destroyed' was actually amended to a 'probable'. However, a He111 of III/KG.55 is believed to have crashed in the Humber that night and it may well have been the bomber claimed by Braham and Wilsden.

Throughout those September nights there was plenty of 'trade' but 29 Squadron's crews had no choice but make use of the AI Mk III sets which were like the curate's egg – only good in parts! The closest anyone got to a real interception occurred when an AI Blenheim, flown by Sgt Fraser with air gunner Sgt Thomas Menage and AI operator AC2 Harold Gilyeat, was ordered to investigate a raid at 0040hrs on September 23. Searchlights surpassed themselves and two enemy aircraft were seen. Sadly both bandits were flying in the opposite direction to and above the Blenheim, so by the time Fraser had turned to intercept, both E/A were out of sight and never seen again and on top of this, the AI set then packed up.

Patrol reports all told the same miserable tale. Blenheims without AI couldn't spot the enemy and those interceptions with AI – assuming the set actually worked – often turned out to be 'friendlies'. Furthermore, there were R/T failures, they were fired on by so-called 'friendly' AA guns, had crash-landings and endured poor searchlight co-operation. Even when it was good, the Blenheims were simply not agile enough to catch up with their targets.

The sharp end of a 29 Squadron Blenheim Mk IF, showing the AI Mk III aerial in the middle of the nose and the four .303in gun pack under the fuselage. (via Martyn Chorlton)

Blenheims were still being detached to support air cover around both Birmingham and Liverpool and patrols were flown over the Point Of Aire on most nights during October. 29 Squadron's aircraft wandered far and wide in search of trade.

At 2050hrs on October 12, one of 29 Squadron's Blenheims was sent off to patrol over Spalding but on reaching his line the pilot was ordered to fly south-west to intercept hostile raids in the Midlands. He saw considerable AA gunfire, bomb explosions and incendiaries in the Coventry area but the complete absence of searchlights made interceptions impossible. At one time control informed this pilot that he was surrounded by no less than 12 enemy aircraft and still he saw nothing!

On a more positive note though, the next night saw Sgts Arthur Roberts and Ronald Mallett on a searchlight co-operation sortie when they observed bombs dropping in the Grantham area. Roberts spotted an enemy aircraft at 13,000ft and followed it down to 3,000ft where he opened fire with his front guns at 500yds. The enemy returned fire but it was wide of the mark and Roberts continued to shoot at the enemy's starboard engine using nearly all 2,400 rounds in the ventral gun-pack. That engine seemed to stop just as the enemy aircraft disappeared into a cloud layer so Sgt Roberts could only claim a 'damaged'.

November 13, 1940 would be remembered for a couple of events of significance. It was the day that Flt Lt Guy Gibson arrived at Digby to take up a flight commander post with 29 Squadron. The same day, Beaufighter R2140 was delivered to the station from Shawbury, followed next day by R2141 from St Athan. Things were looking up indeed! By the end of November, Sqn Ldr Widdows had re-organised the squadron into 'A' Flight with Beaufighters, four pilots and the squadron leader himself and 'B' Flight with Blenheims and nine pilots. Sadly, this re-organisation did not come soon enough for the squadron to have any beneficial impact on the biggest air raid on Coventry on the night of November 14/15. Later that day, Flt Lt Charles Winn and Fg Off Braham went to St. Athan to collect more Beaufighters and, for 29 Squadron, the era of the Blenheim came to an end.

Chapter 10

Blenheims in the East

In 1938, the first overseas squadron to be equipped with the Blenheim Mk I was 30 Squadron based in Iraq. They had arrived by sea in crates from the Packing Depot at Sealand via the Aircraft Depot at Aboukir in late 1937. Once they had been unpacked and assembled, Vokes tropical air filters were fitted to the carburettor intakes, guns were installed and they were then air tested. Deliveries to 30 Squadron at Mosul commenced in January 1938.

This was an important aircraft in the RAF and the fact that it was sent to the Middle East where rather older types held sway – 30 Squadron replaced their Hardys - is an interesting point. Guarding the Suez Canal was paramount and modern aircraft were essential if the RAF were to carry out the task. At this stage in 1938, it was Italy that was a possible nuisance in the area and not (yet) Nazi Germany. Other units were scheduled to receive the Blenheim but it was not until February and March 1939 that another 50 crated examples arrived; these went to 84 and 55 Squadrons – replacing the Vincent – and a month later 211 Squadron exchanged their Hinds for Blenheims. Wellesleys, Westland Wapitis and even Singapore flying boats were replaced with the Blenheim, which was much faster than any of the above.

Desert War

The outbreak of World War Two did not affect the Middle East immediately, it was only after the fall of France and when Italy declared war on Britain on June 10 that the situation altered.

Blenheims over the Pyramids, Egypt, on 30 May 1940.

Italy had a major presence in Libya with over 300,000 troops and some 300-plus aircraft against 36,000 allied troops and fewer than 100 aircraft in the area. There were four squadrons of Blenheims (45, 55, 211 and 113) alongside the Army Co-operation Lysanders and elderly Bombay troop transports that could be used as bombers if required. The RAF Blenheims based in Iraq and Aden were quite some distance away.

Further, Italy was in a better location and could call for reinforcements with ease from Sicily but with the Mediterranean surrounded by the enemy, Britain could not easily protect its interests in the Middle East. The army and RAF in that area would have to accept the burden of protecting those interests. Besides, there were no reinforcements; they were busy defending Britain.

Commanding 202 Group (later the Desert Air Force) was World War One ace – with 60 confirmed victories - Air Cdre Raymond Collishaw. He was a man of action and immediately Italy declared war on Britain he sent six Blenheims on an armed reconnaissance mission over Libya. Collishaw wanted to know where the enemy was and what its strength was. Following the dawn flight on June 11 were eight fully-armed Blenheims from 45 Squadron who bombed the Italian air base at El Adem outside Tobruk. This was a low-level surprise attack that clearly informed the Italians that they had a fight on their hands. The same afternoon, Collishaw sent 18 Blenheims from 55 and 113 Squadrons to raid El Adem once again. Both missions met with success and apart from serious damage to the airfield, not to mention Italian morale, some 20 enemy aircraft were destroyed or damaged. Three Blenheims from the first raid were lost and four others damaged in both raids. With such a small force of aircraft at his disposal, Collishaw believed that attacking the enemy first was the best defence. In this he was not wrong and it had the approval of his AOC, Sir Arthur Longmore.

Collishaw did not let up and on June 12 a force of 28 Blenheims from 45, 55 and 21 Squadrons took-off to bomb the harbour at Tobruk. Unfortunately, the weather was poor and only a few aircraft found and attacked Tobruk; other aircraft bombed targets they spotted en route and four Blenheims landed

30 Squadron, not long after arriving at Ismailia in August 1939, with a Vickers Valencia transport in the foreground. (via Martyn Chorlton)

back at base with their bombs still on board. While there were no RAF losses on the mission, three Blenheims were lost or damaged through accidents on the ground. Further missions against the Italians were mounted and, in the first five days since June 10, Blenheims had flown 106 bombing sorties with varying success. Four aircraft were lost through enemy action and several were damaged but they also shot down Italian fighters and bombed ships and troop positions as well as airstrips.

With his few Blenheims, Collishaw used them wisely but not sparingly; the four Egyptian-based squadrons were used on a daily basis with raids on Italian army posts and airfields. There were three squadrons (45, 55 and 211), equipped with Mk Is and one (113) with Mk IVs. As each day unfolded, fewer aircraft were serviceable but as long as there were Blenheims the attacks continued, even though ACM Longmore queried Collishaw's use of the Blenheim as a low-level strafing aircraft against defended targets. Nevertheless, he did promise reinforcements but these could not be ferried from Britain to Egypt as they would have to fly either over enemy-held territory or take a long arduous route which included a lengthy over-sea crossing. In the event, Blenheims were crated, along with Hurricanes, and sent to Takoradi on the Gold Coast to be re-assembled and flown to Egypt. The first Blenheim arrived via this route in mid-September.

Blenheims and other aircraft began to arrive on a regular basis and soon the older types, such as Wellesleys, had been replaced. This was fortuitous as the Italians, under Marshal Graziani, began to assemble in force to invade Egypt. They halted at Sidi Barrani on September 16 and dug-in. Collishaw's photo-reconnaissance Blenheims had kept a regular watch on Graziani's movements and the information was of great value to General Wavell and the commanders of the British and Commonwealth troops waiting for the battle. Blenheims also bombed and strafed the Italian positions and were later joined by Wellingtons to add to the bombing missions. On December 9, General Richard O'Connor sent his armies in to attack Sidi Barrani and they captured their objective on the 11th and the Italians were chased out of Egypt.

'DOUGH-NUT-DAISY' of 84 Squadron, one of many abandoned at Medini in Greece.

Greek campaign

Although the Italians had been ousted, the threat remained but, because of the need to help Greece, many aircraft and troops were transferred to that theatre. While this was happening, General Erwin Rommel and the Afrika Korps had arrived to take over from the Italians; he wasted no time and on March 24, 1941 launched an attack which resulted in Benghazi falling on April 3. The RAF was caught up in this rapidly changing scene and abandoned airfields as they lost ground. Blenheims of 45 and 55 Squadrons mounted several attacks on the German army and helped to stop their advance on Tobruk. Urgently required were reinforcements, both land and air, if disaster was to be averted.

This was not easy, as the route from Gibraltar through the Mediterranean was treacherous. Enemy submarines were on patrol and any shipping was within reach of Axis aircraft. Additionally, many of the RAF fighters and bombers had been sent to aid in the defence of Greece. Blenheims from 30, 84 and 211 Squadrons were in action during November 1940 bombing Italian targets in Albania. During these raids, which saw the Blenheim as a fighter and a bomber, losses were taken – two aircraft were lost to Italian fighters on November 13 and another was shot down the next day. By the beginning of December, the weather had deteriorated considerably; snow and ice added to the worsening visibility and adverse conditions made it difficult to keep the aircraft serviceable. Nevertheless, sorties continued with regular attacks on Valona harbour and on Italian troop positions along the coast road between Albania and Greece. AVM Arthur Tedder took over command from ACM Longmore and inherited an almost static air force. The winter rains continued and rendered the airfields muddy and waterlogged making operations difficult. The sterling service by the ground-crews must be commended; they worked outdoors in all weathers so that aircraft would be ready for operations. Conditions were poor with all personnel living under canvas in a primitive environment. However, 211 Squadron mounted several missions on Elbasan in early January. They lost one Blenheim and others suffered damage but the Italian positions were bombed despite enemy fighter activity.

Bristol Blenheim Mk I from 113 Squadron flying low-level over British troops in the western desert in 1940.

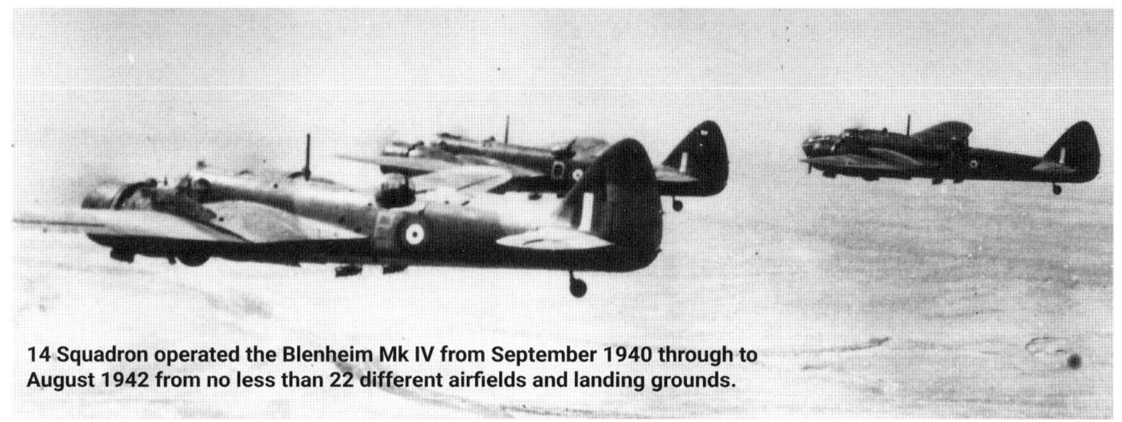

14 Squadron operated the Blenheim Mk IV from September 1940 through to August 1942 from no less than 22 different airfields and landing grounds.

The air war by the RAF to assist the Greeks in their fight against the Italians was fierce but it has been overlooked in histories of the war. Italy invaded Albania and was intent on using that country as a spring board to attack Greece but they did not take into account the formidable fighting prowess of the Greek armed forces, which included 12 Blenheims Mk IVs purchased in 1939. They fought alongside the RAF aircraft and inflicted damage on the enemy but as the battles continued and pushed the Italians back the Germans took an interest. They had been building up forces in the Balkans and by spring 1941 were in a position to aid their Italian ally and attack the Greek positions in force. The RAF was, once again, in the midst of the action.

Germany invaded Greece from Bulgaria and moved quickly before the Greeks – who were heavily involved in fighting the Italians in southern Albania – could react. They could not fight on both fronts and though assisted by their allies it was an uneven fight. RAF Blenheims were sent to bomb German troop positions in Yugoslavia and in the Strumica region with varied success. Reinforcements were required and Tedder sent Blenheims from Egypt to Crete to assist with the escalating battle. The German forces proved numerically superior and the Greeks continued to be pushed back, fighting valiantly all the way. On April 13, Blenheims of 211 Squadron carried out raids on troop positions with some success but when they attempted a third mission later in the day they were intercepted by Messerschmitt Bf109s from JG27 and six of the seven Blenheims were shot down. Sadly, only two aircrew survived.

German aircraft, in turn, raided the bases from which the Blenheims were operating and several aircraft were destroyed or seriously damaged on the ground. As the Germans advanced into Greece the allies withdrew and the RAF flew their remaining aircraft to airfields on the island of Crete; to bolster the defence of the island nine Blenheim Mk IVFs from 203 Squadron were deployed from Aden. They were sorely needed as the enemy turned their attention to Crete. On April 27, the Germans took Athens, and Greece was out of the war; the last of the allied forces withdrew from Greece.

Crete was not forgotten and once the Germans had captured the airfields in southern Greece they could attack the island, which was important for control of that part of the Mediterranean. The Luftwaffe carried out intensive attacks on the allied shipping convoys and on the airfields of Crete. Defending the island were RAF fighters, including Blenheims, but they were seriously outnumbered. Aircraft losses mounted – some to mistaken fire from ships evacuating troops from the island – and the RAF was forced to withdraw. The remaining Blenheims from 11, 30, 84, 113, 203 and 211 Squadrons were flown to various bases in Egypt where they were all in need of repair. Crete was invaded on May 20 by airborne paratroops who secured the airfields, allowing further German troops to land in the days that followed. The last of the allied forces on the island were taken off from the south by the Royal Navy as the enemy was securing the north of the island.

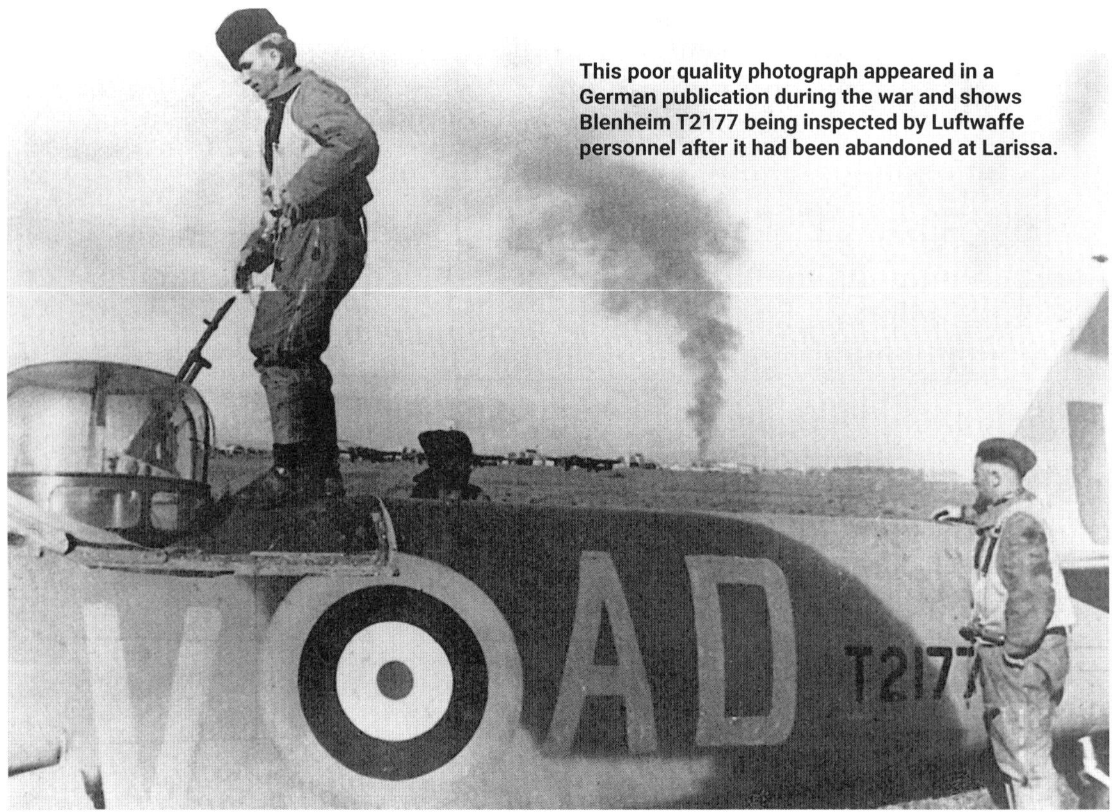

This poor quality photograph appeared in a German publication during the war and shows Blenheim T2177 being inspected by Luftwaffe personnel after it had been abandoned at Larissa.

This did not mark the end of the Blenheims and Crete; they operated from bases in Egypt to harass enemy shipping and even raid the airfields that they had so recently vacated. On May 26 four Blenheims from 45 Squadron were sent to bomb Maleme airfield, they were intercepted by Messerschmitt Bf109s from JG77 and two Blenheims were shot down. Other raids on the airfield followed but few aircraft managed to get to Malema and those that did caused little damage. By the end of May it was obvious that the Blenheims could not continue and the raids were discontinued.

Having fought in the Greek campaign the Blenheims were back in action in the desert war. Germany had come to the aid of their Italian ally and the RAF were busy attacking German positions. Fresh Blenheims had been arriving via Taoradi and by long ferry flight from the UK. The last was hazardous and several aircraft were lost to enemy action.

On July 30 1941, Collishaw handed over 204 Group to AVM Arthur Coningham. Collishaw had done a valiant job but he was tired and needed a rest from operations. The Blenheims of 11, 14, 55, 84, 113 and 203 Squadrons were joined by a detachment of 8 Squadron Blenheims and also by SAAF 15 Squadron Blenheims. They were all fresh aircraft with rested crews who would now take part in Operation Crusader to relieve Tobruk.

General Auchinleck launched the operation on November 18, 1941. Blenheim bombers and fighters attacked enemy supply columns and troop movements on a daily basis. Often the raids by Blenheims and other RAF bombers were made well behind the front line, but at that stage the enemy fighter force was not up to strength and, although the RAF lost aircraft, they enjoyed considerable success. The Germans brought in reinforcements including the large, powerful and experienced Luftflotte II from the eastern front.

Blenheim MK IV T2177 of 113 Squadron at Medini in Greece in 1941 prior to flying a reconnaissance sortie along the Greek/Bulgarian border before the German invasion.

Operation Crusader captured Benghazi on December 24 and the battle continued as the year came to a close. The New Year saw the desert war continue and the Blenheims carrying out bombing and strafing missions on a regular basis. Interestingly, a few aircraft were converted locally to carry a 20mm Hispano cannon in the nose. This was mounted in the observer's position with the ammunition feed and box taking up the rest of the available space. It added firepower to the Blenheim and although the guns often jammed they were effective in the strafing role.

Malta

Blenheims were ferried from Britain to the island of Malta in the Mediterranean. Before the collapse of France, the journey was across France and staged through Suez and on to Malta. With the fall of France, the aircraft were fitted with a 100-gallon auxiliary fuel tank in the bomb bay for the flight from Cornwall to Gibraltar. Here they were refuelled and flown on to Malta. It was a dangerous but vital journey, for the aircraft were required not only in Malta but also for North Africa and the western desert. 21 Squadron was deployed to Malta in April 1941 to carry out bombing missions on enemy shipping taking supplies to the Afrika Korps. They met with some success and denied many a fuel tanker and supply ship that would have assisted the enemy forces. Soon, 82 Squadron joined the Malta Blenheims and they also strafed and bombed the enemy ships. Keeping the aircraft serviceable were the dedicated ground crews who worked under difficult conditions with little cover, shortage of spares and very little rest. Their ceaseless work meant that the RAF continued the fight; in July 110 Squadron arrived and went straight into action. Their aircraft were joined by Blenheims of 105 Squadron under the command of Wg Cdr Hughie Edwards VC, DFC. Blenheims took the fight to the enemy, which was attacking the island with increasing ferocity. The RAF suffered serious casualties and lost several aircraft, many Blenheims among them. However, the AOC of RAF Malta, AVM Hugh Pughe Lloyd MC, DFC found an excellent method of replacing aircraft. When fighters and bombers staged through Malta on their way to the Middle East he retained many as replacements. The aircraft and crews were soon flying missions for RAF Malta.

The battle for Malta was crucial for the Axis forces if they were to succeed in the desert campaign, and that this was denied was down to a small determined force of Royal Navy and RAF personnel who took the battle to the enemy. On the ground in Malta the army kept up their anti-aircraft fire as well as carrying out a myriad of other duties. Above all, the people of Malta never for one moment lost heart or doubted their allies on the island.

In all the actions RAF Blenheims were on constant patrol and flying offensive sweeps to harass enemy shipping and troop movements. For example, on August 11, 1941, two sections of three 105 Squadron aircraft took off to raid a nitrate manufacturing plant in Crotone in Southern Italy. The first flight missed the location and bombed some railway buildings but the second section found and bombed the factory. Anti-aircraft fire from Italian ships moored offshore hit Squadron Leader George Goode's Blenheim as it came in to make a second run; the Blenheim crashed near Crotone and the crew were captured. A second aircraft was also hit and damaged but was able to get back to Luqa on Malta where it crashed on landing.

It was 105 and 107 Squadrons that carried out most of the Blenheim missions, they spent long hours looking for enemy shipping en route to North Africa as well as strafing enemy positions in Libya. Other sorties included an attack on a factory and power station at Licata in Sicily on August 30 when six aircraft from the two squadrons scored several hits. They made a return trip to the factory at Crotone on September 1; seven aircraft flew in at low-level to bomb the chemical works, the railway lines and ships in the harbour. All-in-all it was a successful raid but the missions were taking their toll on aircraft and crews. The late Sir Ivor Broom KCB recalled his time, as a Sergeant pilot, flying Blenheims from Malta. "We carried out all manner of missions and they were sometimes quite long flights. Malta was a sort of aircraft carrier in the Med and from there we could range to the coast of Libya, southern Italy and Sicily. In between were the enemy ships, convoys taking supplies to Rommel. That was what we were after, especially the fuel tankers. If Rommel had no fuel he could not use his vehicles and tanks. I arrived in Malta in early September 1941 so I was there later than those who had been battling for months before. I was supposed to be on my way to Egypt but was effectively 'shanghaied'! My first mission was against the barracks at Homs. Sadly, two aircraft collided, one was the CO, Wing Commander Scivier, and his aircraft crashed, but the other flown by Sergeant Williams made it back having bombed the target." What Broom did not mention was that on the way back to Malta the damaged aircraft was lagging behind and was in a bad way; it had bent propellers and a missing pitot tube following the collision. Consequently, Williams had no way of knowing his airspeed or altitude. Broom went back and escorted the badly vibrating Blenheim back to Luqa, and his observer signalled speed and altitude with an Aldis lamp to the other aircraft. When they approached the runway at Luqa, Broom flew alongside Williams' aircraft to guide him on to the runway before he turned and landed himself.

Ivor Broom flew many more missions and was soon a veteran of the Malta campaign. Blenheims continued their raids but, even though replacements were arriving on a regular basis, losses were mounting due to German fighter action. Renewed efforts by the Axis to conquer Malta meant that additional fire-power was brought in. Germany increased its bombing raids on Malta and many aircraft were destroyed on the ground and so, as numbers decreased, it was decided to move the remaining RAF bombers to safety and in March 1942 the few surviving Blenheims and Wellingtons were flown out of Malta to Egypt.

This photo, taken in Libya, possibly in 1941, shows an aircraft dump filled with Blenheims. Only a 11 Squadron machine is discernible.

Final missions

By this stage, many Blenheims were deployed to the Far East theatre but those that remained in the Middle East continued operations against the Afrika Korps where they were joined or replaced by the new Mk V. Unfortunately, this model was not ideal for desert conditions and serviceability became an issue as did the high loss rate. It should have been clear that the aircraft design was now outdated but with the lack of any modern replacement it soldiered on. Apart from taking part in Operation Torch – the invasion of North Africa – the Mk V carried out several bombing missions against the enemy. For daylight raids, fighters escorted the Blenheims but later in the year when the weather deteriorated they had to fly unescorted.

Blenheims were restricted to night operations and as more modern types arrived in theatre the type was relegated to maritime duties and by the end of 1943 had been replaced by Venturas. Just one squadron (614) continued to use the Mk V on maritime patrols in the Mediterranean until January 1944 when it was disbanded. Production of the Mk V has ceased in June 1943 and the Blenheim was out of front-line service in the Middle East, but it continued in the Far East theatre for many more months.

Ivor Broom, who became a distinguished Mosquito pilot, told me:
"You cannot compare the Mosquito and the Blenheim. They were two quite different aircraft but I will always retain a great fondness for the Blenheim which gave me my first taste of action."

Chapter 11

Norge Patrol

Ex-404 (Buffalo) Squadron RCAF navigator Roger G Napier gives an insight into a typical long-range patrol of the Norwegian coast in late 1941. Kindly supplied by The Blenheim Society.

Sometimes I pause in my work and wonder at it – here I am, suspended between boundless sky and limitless sea, boring on through the rain-swept darkness at an ungodly hour of the night and for what purpose? In the words of the briefing officer: 'To patrol a section of the Norwegian coastal fjords and to report enemy shipping.' 'If any', is what we would like to add to those brief instructions, for this is November of 1941 and the British navy, Coastal and Bomber Commands have by this time taken such a vast toll of enemy shipping that it is rare indeed to sight a ship of any consequence.

I often wonder as I fly if it is worth it – two years ago tonight at this time I would have been in bed or driving home after a merry party, and yet here I am, cramped, cold, uncomfortable and apprehensive, flying in a twin-engined land plane over 380 miles of the stormy North Sea at an average height of 50 feet!

It speaks volumes for our maintenance crews and for the excellence of the aircraft that not many of us do give much thought to the possibility of engine failure.

Soon we come to the edge of the clouds and ahead of us is the long black sprawling mass of the Norwegian coast. We are now in brilliant moonlight for the moon is full and high in the sky. It looks as though we are in the limelight of some vast theatre and that no one could help but see us against the dark wastes of the sea.

A low Scottish sun is close to setting as a 404 (Buffalo) Squadron crew in their Mk IVF prepare for another sortie across the cold North Sea to Norway. (404 Squadron RCAF)

404 Squadron officers, most likely taken at Skitten on October 1, 1941. (Left to right rear row), Doc Ward, Plt Off Hoadley, Plt Off Fletcher, Plt Off Pierce, Plt Off Napier (author), Plt Off Dunlop, Plt Off Mathews, Plt Off Tustin, Doc Kirk. (Left to right front row), Fg Off Crump, Fg Off Munden, Plt Off Foster, Flt Lt Watson, Sqn Ldr Woodruff (Officer Commanding and pilot in 'Norge Patrol'), Flt Lt McHardy, Flt Lt Hay-Roe, Plt Off Inglis, Plt Off Metcalfe and Flt Lt McKenzie. (404 Squadron RCAF)

I am fully keyed up now and feverishly check my position with a large-scale local map. Map reading is extremely difficult at very low altitudes as one sees the profiles rather than the shapes of islands, promontories and bays. Add the eerie effect of the moonlight, and the unseen but well-felt presence of the enemy, and you have a tricky job indeed to pin-point your position. I find that the easiest way is to look at the contours shown on the map, convert them to a sort of mental side-elevation and fit them in with the dark shapes before us.

Tonight I am agreeably surprised to find that, due to a good wind supplied by our meteorological people, and to excellent flying by my skipper 'Woody' Woodruff, my course has been good and that we are less than a mile out in our landfall. Skipping quickly over the first row of coastal islands, we enter the inland waterway where we are most likely to find enemy shipping. We are a scant five miles north of Bergen – reputedly a hot spot for night fighters, flak and searchlights but we turn doggedly south and slide swiftly – very swiftly it seems at that low altitude – over the quiet waters of the fjord.

Woody is tense at the controls for we are travelling now at some two hundred miles per hour through unknown, high-walled and twisty fjords and too close to the water for any relaxation.

Despite being formed at Thorney Island on April 15, 1941 the squadron's crest was not officially presented until 1943 by which time the unit was operating the Beaufighter. (Martyn Chorlton)

Beautiful yet very dangerous

"Hi Joe," I call down the inter-com to the rear gunner, "How's your aerial current?" This is an old joke between us and refers to his other duty of operating the radio set. He spends a lot of time digging into the vitals of his 'museum piece' radio to obtain the necessary aerial current for transmission and hardly ever knows where we are going as a result. He comes back with a succinct, "Nuts to you" and I can see him in my imagination, perched up as high as possible in his turret, gazing intently out over the twin muzzles of his Brownings.

We keep to the west side of the fjord so that we can look down the moon path to the east and thus spot any movement. On we go – "Bear left and then sharp right" I sing out to Woody over the inter-com. I am now pin pointing our way along the map using the moonlight alone as any other light shown in the transparent nose of the aircraft would probably be fatal.

Shortly after we turn the corner, the fjord narrows – it is scarcely half a mile wide – and suddenly a searchlight opens up. He is actually above our level on the high bank of the fjord and apparently is having difficulty in fixing our position, for, although he is following our track, the beam is miles above us.

There are myriads of little winking lighthouses but no ships – or is that one ahead of us to our right? I call to Woody and he swings to starboard. It is a ship, a little one, and I try hard to assess its tonnage, remembering all the instructions, information and suggestions pumped into us for just such an occasion.

I am still trying to 'tape' him as he passes under our starboard engine when suddenly he opens up on us. I involuntarily duck behind the solid part of the nose as streams of red and golden glow-worms go shooting past us. As I sit watching the tracer going by – the red to die far out over the water and the gold to explode with vicious-looking bursts a thousand yards away – momentarily it amuses me to think that I sought shelter from this flak behind a sheet of magnesium about a sixteenth of an inch thick! A sort of human ostrich act!

Nice view of the four-gun belly pack under the fuselage of a 404 Squadron Mk IVF being carefully checked by a pair of RCAF ground crew. (404 Squadron RCAF)

More attentive ground crew service a 404 Squadron Mk IVF on a summer's day at Dyce in 1942. (404 Squadron RCAF)

Woody is taking evasive action now and I grin in the dark as the moonlit water tips up at a sharp angle to us. 'Good old Woody, he's a swell pilot' and 'Nice work Joe', I can hear the sharp staccato bark of the rear guns over the intercom as he replies to the fire. They certainly are a grand team to work with and for. "That stuff was close though and why should something so dangerous look so beautiful – a sort of deadly nightshade I suppose – glad the pigeon in his little yellow can wasn't hit". These and other stray thoughts flit quickly through my mind as I mark the position of the ship on my map.

On we go, banking, turning and twisting through the fjords and, while watching the surface for ships, I cannot help thinking abstractedly of the flap the Germans must be in. I have often been in our own fighter ops room when German raiders were around. 'Type unknown, course so-and-so, he must be heading for such-and-such an objective – no he isn't – where the hell are our fighters'. An orderly chaos of blinking lights, swift-moving WAAFS pushing little lettered stands about on a huge chart – the controller above, with ranks of phones on either side, like some vast spider perturbed by vibrations in his web.

Landfall

I snap back to the present, fervently wishing I could see behind the aircraft yet relying on Joe to do his stuff should any aircraft get on our tail. But we are lucky and at last are heading out to the wide open sea again.

"Phew" – even though we are not absolutely safe for another 80 miles or so, we all relax and I can see Woody grinning at me in the moonlight. I pour him a cup of coffee and hand it back – if his mouth is as dry as mine, he can do with it! Next a couple of sandwiches and more coffee – I have quite a spread

Above: 404 Squadron's popular commanding officer, Sqn Ldr 'Woody' Woodruff at his desk, possibly at Dyce. (404 Squadron RCAF)

Right: A Wireless Operator/Air Gunner climbs into his Mk IVF at Dyce in 1942. (404 Squadron RCAF)

on my navigation table, and the maps are well out of the way in case of any spilt coffee, as Woody periodically swings the aircraft so that Joe can see under and behind the tail.

Now I make out a weather report and after coding and ciphering it, call up Joe on the intercom to come forward for it. I wiggle my arm over the armour plating and finally Joe's strong grip finds mine in the darkness so I can hand him the message and some sandwiches. It is his turn for coffee and 'eats' – he has an important job back there and it is very cold in the turret so he needs it. He can quit peering into the darkness now that we are out of the danger area.

A small yellow blob of light is all that I can have on my nav table and so, as I fill in my log and plot in my tracks on the chart, measure the distance home and calculate the time it will take us, I have to slide my work to and fro under the light like a woman running up a dress on a sewing machine.

The most important part of my work now begins – I have to get us back to base and it is nearly two hours flight. Tonight I am lucky, the clouds have cleared somewhat and the air is steady enough to

Above: 'Woody' Woodruff in more relaxed pose entertaining his men in the Officers' Mess at Dyce. (404 Squadron RCAF)

Right: Pilot, Flt Sgt Brown (right) and his observer Flt Sgt Oliver captured concentrating during a live operational sortie somewhere over the North Sea. (404 Squadron RCAF)

take astro sights. Out with the old bubble sextant, a roar as I open the side window to reduce refraction and then steady, steady. 'Blast Woody, why can't he keep this ruddy kite steady' – as I try to keep the star in the centre of the bubble which is dancing to and fro. Observations of Polaris and a planet, plus two calculations result in two fixes.

'Let's see how it checks with my DR track – hm – not so bad, we'll be north of our track tonight' so, just before our estimated time of arrival, I shall look out for the white 'planet' light flashing 'L', lying to the north of base.

"Hi, Joe, how about a QDM old boy? We'll be in, in half-an-hour or so, ETA 0316hrs." So Joe gets me a bearing which is another check on the navigation. It sometimes happens that, owing to unforeseen winds, this is the only way of getting back, but tonight everything seems to be under control. His bearing differs only slightly from my course, so I relax, give Woody another sandwich and have one myself before staring the business of getting in.

For a navigator this is always the most crucial and exciting part of the trip. On this landfall, other people judge his navigation and the navigator in his own mind judges the met forecast and the ability of his pilot to fly accurately on instruments, for navigation is nothing more or less than straight mathematics plus a certain amount of judgement. Tonight everything is great; and although having covered something like 1,000 miles in five hours, dead ahead of us – just before ETA - comes up a white flashing light.

Relief

Now we can see the faint line of the shore, but as we turn towards the 'drome, we can see nothing of the flare path. Then, as we circle and lose height, and I fire a recognition signal, the red obstruction lights come on and we can suddenly see the flare path – little pin pricks of light invisible from over a thousand feet.

I sigh with relief, close up my log book and strap myself in alongside the pilot; 'Hardly necessary – Woody makes such wizard landings, but just in case!' From now on, it is entirely up to him.

A final circuit: 'Fine pitch, take-off mixture, wheels down, flaps down' – mechanically I check Woody's operations over to myself and then up comes the brilliant flood-lit runway – bump, bump, and we are down.

Tomorrow the papers will carry a note to the effect that: 'Coastal Command carried out a reconnaissance of the Norwegian Coast last night.'

The Blenheim Society

During the late 1980s the idea of forming an association or society to focus the attention of the many people who were interested in the history of the Blenheim aircraft and the personnel connected with it had been considered by several people. For many, the catalyst for this renewed interest was the completion of the 12-year rebuild to flying condition of a Mk IV Blenheim by Graham Warner and his team at the British Aerial Museum at Duxford, particularly after the considerable publicity given to the first flight on 28th May 1987.

From mid-1986 onwards, Hugh George held discussions with other like-minded people and found sufficient interest to justify the formation of a society. It had been hoped the recently restored Blenheim would fly at a reunion arranged at Wyton by Hugh and Betty George on 4th September 1987. Regrettably, the aircraft was written off on 21st June 1987 when it crashed at Denham, which attracted more publicity. Graham Warner took the decision to sponsor the restoration of a second Blenheim to flying condition and declared his intentions at a press conference on 28th June 1987 where the Blenheim Appeal was launched and the proposed formation of The Blenheim Society announced. All interested parties came together on 4th September 1987 at the *Old Bridge Hotel*, Huntingdon where an ad-hoc committee was appointed to formulate the aims of a society and proceed with its formation.

The first public meeting was held on 28th November 1987 at Duxford with an attendance of 300 and it received good press and TV coverage, so The Blenheim Society was launched most successfully. Further public meetings were held at an air display at Duxford on 15th May 1988 and at the RAF Museum Hendon on 24th September 1988. The formal Inaugural General Meeting of The Blenheim Society was held at Hendon on 19th March 1989 when the ad-hoc committee members stood down and were then all elected en-bloc by the members as the formal committee. The three aims of The Blenheim Society, initially adopted at the Huntingdon meeting, were also approved.

The formation of The Blenheim Society and the establishment of a Committee to direct its activities and to develop general interest resulted from the very considerable efforts of a number of people, some of whom have served in an official capacity, others who have remained in the background. The outcome is a well-established, financially healthy and soundly organised Society with three positive and recognised aims:

- To record the history of Blenheim aircraft and crews in RAF service.
- To raise funds and offer expertise to assist in restoring to flying condition the Blenheim (Duxford) Limited's Bristol Blenheim.
- To arrange reunions and other events for Blenheim veterans and others with a common interest.

For Valour in a Blenheim

Thirty-two airmen were awarded the Victoria Cross during the Second World War; three of them went to Blenheim pilots. Two of them were awarded posthumously and each was not only won in three main theatres of the war, Europe, the Middle East and the Far East but also in three different marks of Blenheim.

Hughie Idwal Edwards

Only three Australian-born airmen won the VC during the Second World War; Hughie Idwal Edwards was the first.

His name could not belie the fact that he was the son of Welsh immigrants who made Fremantle, Western Australia their home in 1910. Hughie Edwards was born on August 1, 1914 and was educated at White Gum Valley School and then Fremantle High School before starting work with a shipping agent's office. At the age of 20, he joined the local artillery garrison but, by July 1935, he transferred to

After a 12-year restoration the original Bolingbroke Mk IV-T, purchased in 1979 by Graham Warner, is captured above Blenheim Palace in early June 1987. The aircraft was painted to represent Wg Cdr Hughie Edwards Mk IV V6028 'GB-B'. Sadly, after only being back in the air for just four weeks, the aircraft crashed near Denham on June 21, 1987. (*Aeroplane Monthly*)

Not much time for the bomb-aimer to hit his target at this height! A bomb-aimer's viewpoint from the nose of a Blenheim Mk IV during the raid on Bremen on July 4, 1941.

the RAAF. Edwards carried out his pilot training at Point Cook, gaining his wings in June 1936. Two months later, he was on the move again, this time to Britain following a transfer to the RAF, where he was commissioned on August 21 and posted to 15 Squadron, Abingdon flying the Hind. 90 Squadron at Bicester was his next posting in March 1937 as adjutant and this was the beginning of Edwards' long association with the Blenheim. In August 1938, Edwards was lucky to escape with his life following a Blenheim crash and, after spending nine months in hospital, he returned to flying duties in April 1940.

In February 1941, Edwards found himself on 139 Squadron at Horsham St Faith flying the Blenheim Mk IV on dangerous daylight operations. However, it was to be another short-lived posting as, on May 11, Edwards was promoted to wing commander and transferred to command 105 Squadron at Swanton Morley, also flying the Mk IV. Edwards wasted no time and, leading from the front on June 15, guided six Blenheims towards a convoy

Wg Cdr H I Edwards VC.

of eight merchant vessels near The Hague. Approaching at less than 50ft, Edwards singled out a 4,000 ton ship and, despite relentless enemy fire, pressed home his attack, crippling his quarry in the process. Two weeks later, Edwards was awarded the first of many decorations for his bravery, the DFC; there was much more to come.

Operation *Wreckage*

The inland port of Bremen had been receiving the constant attention of Bomber Command from the night of June 27/28, 1941 under the guise of Operation *Wreckage*. On this night, 73 Wellingtons and 35 Whitleys suffered the highest losses so far, after encountering 'intense night-fighter attacks' for the first time, but of those aircraft that did drop their bombs, it appears they all fell on Hamburg. Blenheims took part in *Wreckage* the following day but all 18 had to turn back because of poor weather. Bremen was attacked again on June 29/30, this time, 69 out of the 106 bombers taking part claimed to have hit the target. The enemy port was set alight again on the nights of July 2/3 and 3/4 but it was a small group of Blenheims, in broad daylight, on July 4, that was determined to make its mark against this dangerous target.

This was to be Edwards 36th operation as he led 15 Blenheims, nine from 105 Squadron and six from 107 Squadron, from Great Massingham towards the highly defended port of Bremen. All were in the air by 0525hrs as they began the 350mile flight across the North Sea. Flying in Blenheim Mk IV V6028 'D', Edwards ordered the formation, which was now down to 12 aircraft after three had to return with technical problems, to close into a tight formation and to descend to just 50ft above the waves. The small formation crossed into Germany, south of Cuxhaven, before turning south towards Bremen which, despite being a port, was located 35 miles inland.

Edwards steered the small force through the outer defences of Bremen, skilfully avoiding tethered balloon cables and power lines. At this point, Edwards broke radio silence and, as briefed, the formation was ordered to spread out and attack their individual targets. It was then every man for himself as they all, hopefully, made their escape. This method of attack was designed to get the crews across the target as quickly as possible before the enemy flak gunners predicted the Blenheims' positions. Regardless, the already experienced flak crews were firing everything they had at the small

62 Squadron preparing to leave Tengah for Alor Star in Northern Malaya on February 8, 1941.

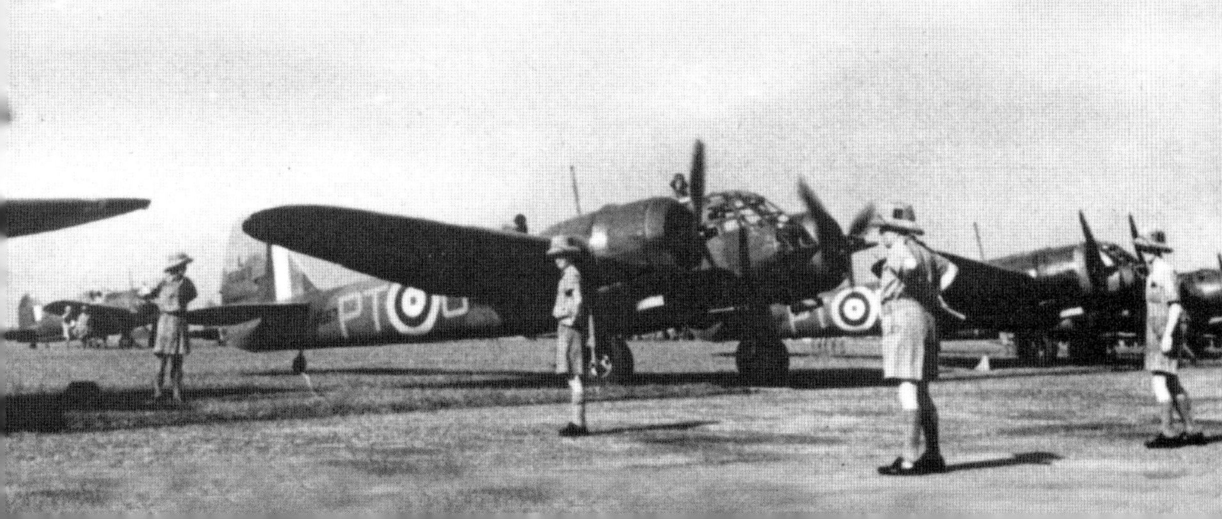

force and in a short space of time three Blenheims had been shot down, one from 105 Squadron and two from 107 Squadron, including the aircraft of Wg Cdr L V E Petley, who, like the others, crashed into the target area.

Edwards' own Blenheim was being thrown around by flak but he managed to focus on his own target in the dock area and release his bombs before continuing on at roof top height across the city towards the outer suburbs. V6028 was under constant fire during the ten-minute-long low run and was hit repeatedly by flak in the bomb bay. At least one shell exploded behind Edwards, seriously wounding his air gunner, Sgt G Quinn DFM.

Rather than immediately running for home, Edwards turned back towards Bremen to observe the rest of his formation also pressing home their attacks. A fourth Blenheim, Z7486, flown by Fg Off M M Lamberts, was trailing smoke and flame as he attempted to clear the port but this was the last anyone saw of the crippled bomber, which is presumed to have crashed not long after. Of the surviving eight Blenheims now making their escape, all were suffering from varying degrees of damage from flak and one flew back to Norfolk trailing a length of severed telegraph cable from its wings and tailplane.

Edwards made his escape via Bremerhaven and Wilhelmshaven before flying over Heligoland and then skimming just above the waves, continued north of the Frisians for 100 miles before turning west towards the Norfolk coast. Back at Swanton Morely just before midday, Edwards' aircraft was the last one down and, after his air

Fg Off (later Sqn Ldr) Arthur Stewart King 'Pongo' Scarf.

gunner was carefully removed from his turret using a Coles crane and hurried to the station's medical quarters, the ground crew began to take in the amount of damage V6028 had sustained. The port wingtip and aileron was missing, the radio had been shattered by a cannon shell, there were telegraph wires wrapped around the tail wheel and the bottom of the fuselage looked like Swiss cheese!

Of those who survived this extraordinarily dangerous operation, four were awarded DFMs, another the DFC and Sgt Quinn gained a bar to his DFM. But the ultimate accolade was bestowed on Wg Cdr Edwards who was awarded the VC for 'the highest possible standard of gallantry and determination'.

Edwards' RAF career continued on an upward spiral and he remained in the service until September 1963, by which time he had become Australia's most decorated airman. Air Cdr Sir Hughie Edwards VC, KCMG, CB, DSO, OBE, DFC passed away in New South Wales on August 5, 1982.

Arthur Stewart King Scarf

Born in Wimbledon on June 14, 1913, Arthur Stewart King Scarf was known to his family as 'John' and, after joining the RAF in January 1936, was called 'Pongo' by his many military friends. Accepted for pilot training, Scarf passed through the AST at Hamble, then 9 FTS, Thornaby, gaining his wings on October 11, 1936.

He was then posted to 9 Squadron at Scampton who were flying the Heyford but by March 1937 he found himself on 61 Squadron at Hemswell flying the Hind. Only a month later, Scarf was posted again to help form a new unit, 62 Squadron, at Abingdon. At first, the new squadron flew the Hind but, after being moved to Cranfield in June 1937, the unit began to re-equip with the Blenheim Mk I.

Posting to the Far East

In August 1939, 62 Squadron was posted to the Far East and Scarf, flying in Blenheim Mk I L1258, along with his colleagues began the long flight via India, eventually arriving at Tengah in Singapore. By early 1941, the allies were becoming concerned about the possibility of Japan entering the war and, in February, 62 Squadron was moved north to Alor Star airfield in the Kedah Province of Malaya, only 20 miles from the neutral Siam border. Despite its neutrality, this was the expected route of a future Japanese invasion and 62 Squadron was positioned right in its path. As predicted, the Japanese invasion began on December 8, 1941 on the beach at Kota Bahru on the east coast of Siam (now Malaysia). The RAF reacted quickly but the five squadrons ordered to attack the invaders missed the main target because of heavy rainstorms, but they did manage to bomb several enemy barges and landing craft. By noon, Siam had fallen and the Japanese began to fly in vast numbers of fighters and bombers into Singora and Patani airfields bringing the whole of Malaysia and Singapore within range. At Alor Star, the 62 Squadron Blenheims had just been refuelled and rearmed as 30 Japanese bombers attacked. After the attack, only two Blenheims remained in a flyable condition but through the tireless efforts of the squadron's ground crew a few more were patched up and, the following day, these were all flown 45 miles south to Butterworth airfield.

Navigator/Observer Flt Sgt 'Paddy' Calder.

Wireless Op/Air Gunner Flt Sgt Cyril Rich

Lone attack on Singora

In retaliation for these attacks, the RAF was ordered to bomb the two occupied airfields at Singora and Patani on December 9. The remnants of 62 and 34 Squadron's Blenheims at Tengah were detailed for the operations, the latter carrying out their raid first with just six Blenheims against Patani. A promised fighter escort never materialised and 34 Squadron lost three aircraft, the survivors landing at Butterworth. The second raid, planned for 1700hrs, was to be a combined 24 and 62 Squadron attack on Singora and the first aircraft away was that of Sqn Ldr Scarf in Blenheim Mk I L1334 'PT-F' with Flt Sgt F Calder flying as navigator and Flt Sgt C Rich in the dorsal turret. Unfortunately, as Scarf circled the airfield waiting for his colleagues to get airborne, a formation of Japanese bombers struck, destroying virtually all of the bombed up Blenheims on the ground.

Scarf could do nothing but pray that some of the Blenheims might have escaped the onslaught but, as the minutes passed, he realised that he was alone. Rather than abandoning the mission, rage took over at the thought of his friends being killed and he decided to continue the attack on Singora alone which by now was over 30 miles inside Japanese territory.

Scarf kept his bomber low but this did not stop several attacks from Japanese fighters which, combined with some skilful flying and some well-aimed fire from Rich's single .303 Lewis machine gun, kept the enemy at bay. As the Blenheim crossed the Siamese border, more fighters arrived, but Scarf stuck to the task and attacked Singora in one steady pass while Rich opened fired into rows of Japanese aircraft parked '….like a row of taxis.' Once the bombing run was over, Scarf turned for home, only to run into another dozen enemy fighters who were determined to finish the Blenheim off. Flying at tree top level and jinking between the many large limestone outcrops unique to the area, Scarf continually managed to shake off each attack while Rich emptied 17 drums of .303in ammunition with short accurate bursts of fire. The enemy fighters were finding their mark though and, the Blenheim was continually hit by cannon and machine gun fire.

It was only a matter of time before the crew began to soak up some of the enemy fire and it was Scarf, in his unarmoured seat, who was hit the most. A single burst of fire hit the left-handed pilot, shattering his left arm, while further rounds passed through his seat into his back. Falling forward over the controls, Calder shouted to Rich for help who unhesitatingly left his turret, put his arm across Scarf's chest and held him back in his seat. Scarf remained conscious and continued to steer the damaged bomber on a southerly course while the Japanese fighters left the Blenheim to its fate.

A few minutes later, the crippled Blenheim appeared over Alor Star airfield, where Scarf attempted to land. Near to the airfield was Alor Star Hospital where Scarf's wife Sally worked as an Army Sister so that she could be near to her husband after they had married in April 1941. Meanwhile, with Rich still keeping Scarf upright and Calder helping his pilot to grip the control column, the bomber approached at 300ft. After lowering the flaps and the undercarriage, the wheels were retracted and the Blenheim belly-landed onto some mud-banked rice paddy field skimming across the surface until the bomber came to a halt in two feet of water, just 100 yards from the hospital.

Both Rich and Calder lifted their wounded skipper from the cockpit onto the wing and, despite the air being filled with petrol fumes, promptly all lit up a cigarette while a small army of hospital staff made their way towards them. Lifted onto a stretcher and administered morphia, Scarf remained conscious and cheerful as he was hurriedly taken to the hospital. Doctors wanted to operate straight away on Scarf's shattered arm, but the brave pilot's loss of blood made a transfusion a higher priority. One of the donors was his wife, who walked with her husband as they wheeled him into the operating

Line of Blenheim Mk Vs at Canrobert airfield in Algeria. (via Martyn Chorlton)

theatre. Sadly, he died only a few minutes later, his weakened body unable to take any more.

Following the subsequent evacuation of Malaya, all documents and records were destroyed and it was not until 1946 that Scarf's incredible story came to light. On June 21, 1946, 'Pongo' Scarf was awarded a posthumous VC and his wife received the award on July 30.

Hugh Gordon Malcolm

Fg Off (later Wg Cdr) Hugh Gordon Malcolm VC.

Born in Broughton Ferry, Dundee, on May 2, 1917, Hugh Gordon Malcolm joined the RAF on January 9, 1936. Passing through the RAF College at Cranwell, Malcolm gained his wings in December 1937 and the same month was posted to 26 Squadron at Catterick flying the Lysander. At the beginning of the war, Malcolm passed through several different units before being appointed as a flight commander in 18 Squadron at Wattisham, flying the Blenheim Mk IV in April 1942. The squadron were heavily involved in night intruder operations and even main Bomber Command operations. The squadron contributed to the first '1,000 bomber' raid in May. The squadron saw out its day with the Blenheim Mk IV in Bomber Command service in August. Declared non-operational, the squadron not only awaited new equipment but also a move overseas. After moving to West Raynham, the new equipment turned out to be the unpopular Blenheim Mk V but, in September, Malcolm was promoted to wing commander, becoming the squadron's new commanding officer which was received with far more enthusiasm. By October, 18 Squadron, along with 13, 114 and 614, had been selected to help support the forthcoming Operation Torch under 326 Wing and all were settled at Blida, Algeria by early November 1942.

Massacre over Chougui

On November 17, 1942, Wg Cdr Malcolm led his unit's Blenheim Mk Vs into action for the first time in an attack on Bizerta airfield. Carried out in daylight and at low level without fighter escort was no place for the Mk V and, after running into bad weather on their return, two Blenheims collided and two more were shot down by German fighters. Bizerta was attacked again eleven days later, this time more successfully, with Malcolm leading the way by making several strafing passes over the target.

On December 4, eleven Blenheims from 326 Wing were moved to a forward airfield at Souk-el-Arba for tactical support operations in support of Allied troops. At 0915hrs, Malcolm led six Blenheim Mk Vs in search of enemy troops in the Chougui area but instead attacked an enemy airfield ten miles north. After returning to Canrobert to refuel, all eleven Blenheims returned to Souk-el-Arba to await further orders. These duly came one hour after landing, calling for the Blenheims to return to the same area they had just attacked, which would mean another daylight attack without fighter escort.

Eleven Blenheim Mk Vs were readied for the operation and at 1515hrs were led from Souk-el-Arba by Wg Cdr Malcolm, flying BA875 'W' of 18 Squadron, with Plt Off J Robb navigating and Plt Off J Grant DFC as wireless operator/air gunner. On take-off, one Blenheim burst the tyre of its tail wheel and slew off the runway, while the remaining ten tucked together in close formation. Twenty minutes later, BA825 of 614 Squadron developed engine trouble and was forced to crash land 15 miles east of Souk-el-Arba. The crew escaped uninjured. With Malcolm still firmly in the lead, he now had four Mk Vs from 13 Squadron and four from 614 Squadron close behind him. As the formation entered the battle zone, enemy observers alerted the closest Luftwaffe airfield and Gruppen I and II of JG 2 were in the air in no time to intercept the Blenheims.

Once Malcolm had reached their objective, the small force began their bombing runs but were immediately 'bounced' by over 50 Bf109s, which quickly tore into the Blenheims. The Mk Vs stood no chance as, one by one, they were sent plunging into the desert in flames. The Luftwaffe later claimed to have shot down all nine Blenheims that day, although it later transpired that three managed to struggle back to Allied lines where they all crash landed. It is most likely that Malcolm's Blenheim was the last to be shot down that day, crashing in flames 15 miles west of the target. Three Allied soldiers found the wreckage of BA875 and, despite the intense heat, managed to remove the body of Plt Off Robb while Malcolm and Grant, most likely already dead, were consumed by the flames.

Wg Cdr Malcolm's courage and determination to carry out his duty regardless of the danger and odds stacked against him led to him being posthumously awarded the VC on April 27, 1943.

Chapter 13

The Blenheim in Service

Royal Air Force (RAF)

6 Squadron
Oculi exercitus
(The eyes of the Army)
A/c: Mk IV Nov '41 to Jan '42
Code: JV Sep '39 to Jul '43

8 Squadron
Uspiam et Passim (Everywhere unbounded)
A/c: Mk I May '39 to Sep '41,
Mk IV Aug '41 to May '42, Mk V
Code: YO Apr '39 to Sep '39,
HV Sep '39 to 1940
Honours: East Africa 1940-41

11 Squadron
Ociores acrioresque aquilis
(Swifter and keener than eagles)

A/c: Mk I Jul '38 to Jan '41,
Mk IV Jan '41 to Aug '43
Code: OY Apr '39 onwards?
YH Sep '39 to 1943
Honours: East Africa 1940; Egypt and Libya 1940-'42; Greece 1941; Syria 1941; Ceylon Apr 1942; Arakan 1943/'44.

13 Squadron
Adjuvamus tuendo
(We assist by watching)
A/c: Mk IV Jul '41 to Sep '42,
Mk V Sep '42 to Dec '43
Code: OO to Nov '42
Honours: Dieppe; North Africa 1942-'43, Mediterranean 1943.

14 Squadron
(I spread my wings and keep my promise)
A/c: Mk IV Sep '40 to Aug '42

Honours: East Africa 1940-41, Egypt and Libya 1941-42, Mediterranean 1941-'43.

15 Squadron
(Aim Sure)
A/c: Mk IV Dec '39 to Oct '40
Code: LS Sep '39 to Apr '51
Honours: France and Low Countries 1939-'40, Mense Bridges, Dunkirk, Invasion Ports 1940, Fortress Europe 1941-'44.

18 Squadron (Burma)
Animo et Fide
(With courage and faith)
A/c: Mk I May '39 to May '40,
Mk IV Mar '40 to Sep '42,
Mk V Sep '42 to Apr '43
Code: GU May '39 to Sep '39,
WV Sep '39 to Oct '42
Honours: France and Low

An 8 Squadron Mk V, BA612, one of several which took part in attacks against Italian East Africa. (via Martyn Chorlton)

Countries 1940, Invasion Ports 1940, Fortress Europe 1940-'42, Channel and North Sea 1940-'41, German Ports 1940-'41, Malta 1941-'42, Egypt and Libya 1942, North Africa 1942-'43.

21 Squadron

Viribus vincimus
(By strength we conquer)

A/c: Mk I Aug '38 to Sep '39,
Mk IV Sep '39 to Mar '42 and Mar '42 to Jul '42

Code: JP Apr '39 to Sep '39,
YH Sep '39 to Nov '47

Honours: Channel and North Sea 1939-'41, France and Low Countries 1940, Dunkirk, German Ports 1941, Fortress Europe 1940-'45, Biscay Ports 1941, Biscay 1941, Malta 1942, Mediterranean 1942.

23 Squadron

Semper agressus
(Always on the attack)

A/c: Mk IF Dec '38 to Apr '41

Code: MS Sep '38 to Sep '39,
YP Sep '39 to May '45

Honours: Channel and North Sea 1939-'41, Fortress Europe 1940-'44.

25 Squadron

Feriens tego (Striking I defend)

A/c: Mk IF Dec '38 to Jan '43

Code: RX Dec '38 to Sep '39,
ZK Sep '39 to Apr '51

Honours: Channel and North Sea 1939-'41, Battle of Britain 1940, Fortress Europe 1943-'44, Home Defence 1940-'45.

27 Squadron

Quam celerime ad astra
(With all speed to the stars)

A/c: Mk IF Feb '41 to Feb '42

Code: PT Sep '39 to Feb '42,
EG Dec '41 to Feb '42

Honours: Malaya 1941-'42, Arakan 1942-'44.

29 Squadron

Impiger et acer (Energetic and Keen)

A/c: Mk IF Dec '38 to Mar '43

Code: YB Dec '38 to Sep '39,
RO Sep '39 to Apr '51

Honours: Channel and North Sea 1939-'40, Battle of Britain 1940, Home Defence 1940-'45.

30 Squadron

Ventre à terre (All out)

A/c: Mk I Jan '38 to Mar '41,
Mk IF Jun '40 to May '41

Code: DP Apr '39 to Sep '39,
VT Sep '39 to Jun '41,
RS Jun '41 to Apr '47

Honours: Egypt and Libya 1940-42, Greece 1940-'41, Mediterranean 1940-'41, Ceylon Apr '42.

34 Squadron

Lupus vult, lupus volat (Wolf wishes, wolf flies)

A/c: Mk I Jul '38 to Nov '41,
Mk IV Jun '41 to Feb '42 and Apr '42 to Jan '43,
Mk V Dec '42 to Jul '43

Code: LB Apr '39 to Aug '39,
EG Sep '39

Honours: Eastern Waters 1941, Malaya 1941-'42, Arakan 1942-'44.

Nice line of 21 Squadron Mk Is at Watton in April 1939. (via Martyn Chorlton)

35 Squadron

(Madras Presidency)
Uno animo agimus (We act with one accord)
A/c: Mk IV Nov '39 to Apr '40
Code: WT Apr '39 to Sep '39

39 Squadron

Die Noctuque (By day and night)
A/c: Mk I Jun '39 to Jan '41, IV Dec '40 to Jan '41
Code: SF Apr '39 to Sep '39, XZ Sep '39 to Dec '40
Honours: East Africa 1940, Egypt and Libya 1940-'43.

40 Squadron

Hostem acoelo expellere (To drive the enemy from the sky)
A/c: Mk IV Dec '39 to Nov '40
Code: BL Sep '39 to Apr '47

42 Squadron

Fortiter in re (Bravely in action)
A/c: Mk V Feb '43 to Oct '43
Code: AW 1943 to Dec 1945
Honours: Pacific 1943-'45, Eastern Waters 1943, Arakan 1943-'44.

44 Squadron (Rhodesia)

Fulmina regis iusta
(The King's thunderbolts are righteous)
A/c: Mk I Dec '37 to Feb '39
Code: JW Oct '38 to Sep '39

45 Squadron

Per ardua surgo (Through difficulties I arise)
A/c: Mk I Jun '39 to Feb '41, Mk IV Feb '41 to Aug '42, Mk IVF May '41 to Jan '42
Code: DD Apr '39 to Sep '39, OB Sep '39 to May '55
Honours: Egypt and Libya 1940-'42, East Africa 1940, Syria 1941, Burma 1942.

52 Squadron

Sudore quam sanguinen (By sweat and blood)
A/c: Mk IV Oct '42 to Feb '43

53 Squadron

(United in effort)
A/c: Mk IV Jan '39 Aug '41
Code: TE Jan '39 to Sep '39, PZ Sep '39 to Feb '43
Honours: France and Low Countries 1939-'40, Dunkirk, Invasion Ports 1940, Channel and North Sea 1940-'44, Fortress Europe 1940-'41, Biscay Ports 1941-'42.

55 Squadron

Nil nos tremefacit (Nothing makes us afraid)
A/c: Mk I Mar '39 to Dec '40, Mk IV Dec '40 to Jun '41 and Aug '41 to Mar '42
Code: GM Apr '39 to Sep '39
Honours: Egypt and Libya 1940-'43.

L1413, a Mk I of 34 Squadron at rest at Upper Heyford in August 1938. (via Martyn Chorlton)

57 Squadron

Corpus non animum muto (I change my body, not my spirit)

A/c: Mk I Mar '38 to May '40
Mk IV Mar '40 to Nov '40

Code: EQ Nov '38 to Sep '39
DX Apr '40 to Apr '51

Honours: France and Low Countries 1939-'40, Norway 1940, Channel and North Sea 1940.

59 Squadron

Ab uno disce omnes (From one learn all)

A/c: Mk IV May '39 to Aug '41

Code: PJ Sep '38 to Sep '39
TR Sep '39 to Oct '42

60 Squadron

Per ardua ad aethera tendo (I strive through difficulties to the sky)

A/c: Mk I Mar '39 to Feb '42
Mk IV Mar '42 to Aug '43
Mk V

Code: AD Apr '39 to Sep '39
MU 1940-'41

Honours: North West Frontier 1935-39, Burma 1941-'42, Malaya 1941-42, Arakan 1942-'44.

61 Squadron

Per purum tonantes (Thundering through the clear air)

A/c: Mk I Jan '38 to Mar '39

Code: 61 Mar 37 to Mar '39

62 Squadron

Insperato (Unexpectedly)

A/c: Mk I Feb '38 to Jan '42

Code: 62 May 37 to Nov '38
JO Nov '38 to Sep '39
PT Sep '39 to Feb '42

64 Squadron

Tenax propositi (Firm of purpose)

A/c: MK IF Dec '38 to Apr '40, Mk IVF

Code: XQ Feb '39 to Sep '39
SH Sep '39 to Apr '51

Honours: Channel and North Sea 1940, Dunkirk, Battle of Britain, Home Defence 1940.

68 Squadron

Vždy Připaven (Always ready)

A/c: MK IF Jan '41 to May '41
Mk IVF

Code: WM '41 to '45

69 Squadron

(With vigilance we serve)

A/c: Mk IV '41

82 Squadron
(United Provinces)

Super Omnia ubique (Over all things everywhere)

A/c: Mk I Mar '38 to Sep '39
Mk IV Aug '39 to Mar '42

Code: OZ Nov '38 to Sep '39
UX Sep '39 to Mar '46

K7130 and K7183 'M' of 44 Squadron on a training sortie out of Waddington in February 1938.

83 Squadron

(Strike to defend)

A/c: Mk I Sep to Oct '38

84 Squadron

Scorpiones pungunt

(Scorpion's sting)

A/c: Mk I Feb '39 to Apr '41
Mk IF, Mk IV Mar '41 to Mar '42, Mk IVF

Code: UR Apr '39 to Sep '39
VA Sep '39 to Mar '41

Honours: Egypt and Libya 1940-'42, Greece 1940-'41, Iraq 1941, Habbaniya, Syria 1941, Malaya (1942?)

86 Squadron

Ad libertates volamus

(We fly to freedom)

A/c: Mk IV Dec '40 to Jun '41

Code: BX Dec '40 to Aug '42

88 Squadron (Hong Kong)

En garde (Be on your guard)

A/c: Mk I Feb '41 to Aug '41
Mk IV Jul '41 to Feb '42

Code: RH Sep '39 to Apr '45

90 Squadron

Celer (Swift)

A/c: Mk I May 37 to Apr '39
and Sep '39 to Apr '40,
Mk IV Mar '39 to Apr '40

Code: TW Oct '38 to Sep '39
WP May '41 to Sep '50

92 Squadron

Aut pugna aut morer

(Either fighter or die)

A/c: Mk IF Oct '39 to Mar '40

Code: GR Oct '39 to May '40
QJ May '40 to Dec '46

Honours: Home Defence 1940-'41, France and Low Countries 1940.

101 Squadron

Mens agitat molem

(Mind over matter)

A/c: Mk I Jun '38 to Apr '39
Mk IV Apr '39 to Jul '41

Code: 101 1935 to Aug '38
LU Apr '39 to Sep '39
SR Sep '39 to Apr '51

Honours: Fortress Europe 1940-'44, Invasion Ports 1940, Ruhr 1940-'45, Berlin 1941, Channel and North Sea 1941-'44, Biscay Ports 1941-'44, German Ports 1941-'44.

104 Squadron

(Strike Hard)

A/c: Mk I May '38 to Apr '40
Mk IV Nov '39 to Apr '40

Code: 104 Jan 36 to Apr '39
PO Apr '39 to Sep '39
EP Sep '39 to Apr '40

105 Squadron

Fortis in præliis

(Valiant in battles)

A/c: Mk IV Jun '40 to Dec '41

Code: 105 1937 to Oct '38
MT Oct '38
GB Sep '39 to Jan '46

A 614 (County of Glamorgan) Mk V being prepared for an operation at dawn from Canrobert. (via Martyn Chorlton)

107 Squadron

Nous y serons (We shall be there)

A/c: Mk I Aug '38 to Jun '39

        Mk IV May '39 to Feb '42

Code: 107 Aug 36 to Oct '38

        BZ Oct '38 to Sep '39

        OM Sep '39 to Oct '48

108 Squadron

Viribus contractis
(With gathered strength)

A/c: Mk I Jun '38 to Apr '40

        Mk IV Oct '39 to Apr '40

Code: 108 Jan 37 to Oct '38, MF

        Oct '38 to Apr '39, LD

        Sep '39 to Apr '40

110 Squadron
(Hyderabad)

Nec timeo nec sperno
(I neither fear nor despise)

A/c: Mk I Jan '38 to Sep '39

        Mk IV Jun '39 to Jun '42

        Mk VE Sep '39 to

        Mar '42

Code: AY Oct '38 to Sep '39

Honours: Channel and North Sea 1939-'42, Norway 1940, France and Low Countries 1940, Dunkirk, Invasion Ports 1940, Ruhr 1940-41, German Ports 1940-'41, Fortress Europe 1940-'42, Malta 1941, Mediterranean 1941.

113 Squadron

Velox et Vindex
(Swift to vengeance)

A/c: Mk I Jun '39 to Apr '40

        Mk IV Mar '40 to Apr '41

        and May '41 to Dec '42

        Mk IVF, Mk V Oct '42 to

        Aug '43

Code: BT Apr '39 to Sep '39

        Mk VA Sep '39 to

        Sep '43

114 Squadron (Hong Kong)

(With speed I strike)

A/c: Mk I Mar '37 to May '39

        Mk IV May '39 to Sep '42

        Mk V Sep '42 to Apr '43

Code: 114 Mar 37 to Apr '39

        FD Apr '39 to Sep '39

        RT Sep '39 to Nov '42

Honours: France and Low Countries 1939-'40, Ruhr 1940-'42, Invasion Ports 1940, Biscay Ports 1940, Channel and North Sea 1940-'42, German Ports 1940-'42, Fortress Europe 1940-'42, North Africa 1942-'43, Mediterranean 1942-'43.

139 Squadron (Jamaica)

Si placet necamus
(We destroy at will)

A/c: Mk I Jul '37 to Sep '39

        Mk IV Jul '39 to Dec '41

        Mk V Jun '42 to Nov 42

Code: SY Apr '39 to Sep '39

        XD Sep '39 to Mar '42

        and Jun '42 to 1951

Honours: France and Low Countries 1939-'40, Channel and North Sea 1940-'41, Fortress

A quartet of 110 Squadron Mk Is carefully sheeted and picketed down during an exercise from their Wattisham home. (via Martyn Chorlton)

Europe 1940-'44, Invasion Ports 1940, German Ports 1941-'45, Biscay Ports 1941-'45, Eastern Waters 1942.

140 Squadron (Foresight)

A/c: Mk IV Sep '41 to Aug '43
Code: ZW Aug '41 to Feb '42

141 Squadron

Caedimus Noctu (We slay by night)
A/c: Mk IF Nov '39 to May '40
Code: TW

143 Squadron

Vincere est vivere
(To conquer is to live)
A/c: Mk IV Dec '41 to Sep '42
Code: HO Jun '41 to Aug '43

144 Squadron

(Who shall stop us)
A/c: Mk I Aug 37 to Apr '39
    Mk V

Code: NV Apr '39 to Sep '39
    PL Sep '39 to May '45

145 Squadron

Diu noctuque pugnamus
(We fight by day and night)
A/c: Mk IF Oct '39 to May '40
Code: SO Apr '39 to Feb '42

162 Squadron

(One time, one purpose)
A/c: Mk IV Feb '42 to Jul '42
    Mk V Jul 42 to Jan '44
Code: GK

173 Squadron

Quocumque (Whithersoever)
A/c: Mk IV Jul '42 to Sep '43

203 Squadron

Occidens oriensque
(West and East)
A/c: Mk I Mar '40 to May '40
    Mk IV May '40 to Nov '42

    Mk IVF, Mk V Oct '42 to Nov '42
Code: CJ, NT
Honours: East Africa, 1940-'41, Mediterranean 1941-'43, Iraq 1941, Habbaniya, Syria 1941, Egypt and Libya 1941-'42.

211 Squadron

Toujours a propos
(Always at the right moment)
A/c: Mk I Apr '39 to Nov '41
    Mk IV May '41 to Feb '42
Code: AO Oct '38 to Mar '39
    LJ Apr '39 to Sep '39
    UQ Sep '39 to Feb '42

218 Squadron (Gold Coast)

(In time)
A/c: Mk IV Jul '40 to Nov '42
Code: HA Sep '39 to Aug '45

219 Squadron (Mysore)

(From dusk till dawn)
A/c: Mk IF Oct '39 to Jun '41

Nice vic formation of Mk IVs of 139 Squadron over France in the winter of 1939/1940. (via Martyn Chorlton)

Code: AM Apr to Sep '39
FK Oct '39 to Sep '46

222 Squadron (Natal)

Pambili bo (Go straight ahead)
A/c: Mk IF Oct '39 to Mar '40
Code: UP Apr '39 to Sep '39
ZD Oct '39 to '53

223 Squadron

Alae defendant Africam
(Wings defend Africa)
A/c: Mk I Jun '41 to Jan '42
Code: AO

226 Squadron

Non sibi sed patroe (For country
not for self)
A/c: Mk IV May '41 to Dec '41
Code: MQ Sep '39 to May '45

229 Squadron (Be bold)

A/c: Mk IF Oct '39 to Mar '40
Code: DB Apr '39 to Sep '39
RE Oct '39 to May '41

233 Squadron

Fortis et fidelis (Strong and
faithful)
A/c: Mk IV Oct '39 to Jan '40
Code: ZS Sep '39 to Jul '42

234 Squadron
(Madras Presidency)

Ignem mortemque despuimus
(We spit fire and death)
A/c: Mk IF Oct '39 to Mar '40
Code: AZ Oct '39 to
Mar '40

235 Squadron

Jaculamur Humi
(We strike them to the ground)
A/c: Mk IF
Mk IVF Feb '40 to
Dec '41
Code: LA Oct '39 to Sep '42

236 Squadron

Speculati Nuntiate
(Having watched, bring word)

A/c: Mk IF Nov '39 to Jul '40
Mk IVF Jul '40 to Feb '42
Code: FA Oct '39 to 41
ND 41 to Aug '43

244 Squadron

A/c: Mk IV Apr '42 to Dec '42
Mk V Oct '42 to Apr '44

245 Squadron
(Northern Rhodesian)

Fugo non fugio
(I put to flight; I do not flee)
A/c: Mk IF Nov '39 to
Mar '40
Code: DX Apr '39 to
Mar '40

248 Squadron

Il Faut en Finir
(It is necessary to make
an end to it)
A/c: Mk IF Dec '39 to May '40
Mk IVF Mar '40 to Jul '41
Code: WR Oct '39 to Oct '43

A 229 Squadron Mk IF photographed over Lincolnshire during a sortie out of Digby. (via Martyn Chorlton)

252 Squadron

(With or on)

A/c: Mk IF Dec '40 to Apr '41
      Mk IVF Dec '40 to
      Apr '41
Code: PN Nov '40 to May '41

254 Squadron

Fljuga vakta ok Ijosta (to fly, to
watch and to strike)

A/c: Mk IF Nov '39 to Apr '40
      Mk IVF Jan '40 to
      Aug '42
Code: QY Oct '39 to Jul '42

272 Squadron

(On, on!)

A/c: Mk IVF Nov '40 to
      Apr '41
Code: XK Nov '40 to May '41

285 Squadron

Respice finem (Consider the end)
A/c: Mk I Dec '41 to Feb '42
Code: VG Dec '41 to Jul '45

287 Squadron

C'est en forgeant (Practice makes
perfect)

A/c: Mk IV Nov '41 to Jan '42
Code: KZ Nov '41 to Jun '46

288 Squadron

(Honour through deeds)

A/c: Mk IV Nov '41 to Feb '42
Code: RP Nov '41 to Jun '46

289 Squadron

A/c: Mk I
      Mk IV Nov '41 to Jan '42
Code: YE Nov '41 to Jun '45

500 Squadron

(County of Kent)

Quo fata vocent (Whither the fates
may call)

A/c: Mk IV Apr '41 to Nov '41
Code: MK Sep '39 to Nov '42
Honours: Channel and North
Sea 1939-'41, Biscay Ports 1941,
Atlantic 1941-'42.

516 Squadron

A/c: Mk IV May '43 to
      Dec '44

521 Squadron

A/c: Mk IV Jul '42 to Mar '43
Code: 5O 42 to '46

526 Squadron

A/c: Mk IV Jun '43 to May '45
Code: MD Jun '43 to May '45

527 Squadron

(Silently we serve)

A/c: Mk IV Jun '43 to May '45
Code: WN Jun '43 to Apr '46

528 Squadron

A/c: Mk IV Jun '43 to Sep '44

600 Squadron (City of London)

Praeter sescentos (More than six
hundred)

A/c: Mk IF Sep '38 to Oct '41
      Mk IVF Nov '39 to
      Jun '40

**Mk IVFs of 235 Squadron bask in the sun at Bircham
Newton in the summer of 1940. (via Martyn Chorlton)**

Code: MV Jan '39 to Sep '39
BQ Sep '39 to Aug '43
Honours: Home Defence 1940-'42,
France and Low Countries 1940

601 Squadron
(County of London)
no motto
A/c: Mk IF Jan '39 to Feb '40
Mk IVF
Code: YN Jan '39 to Sep '39
UF Sep '39 to Apr '42
Honours: France and Low
Countries 1940

604 Squadron
(County of Middlesex)
Si vis pacem, para bellum (If you
want peace, prepare for war)
A/c: Mk IF '39 to May '41
Code: WQ Jan '39 to Sep '39
NG Sep '39 to Apr '45
Honours: France and Low
Countries 1940, Dunkirk, Battle of

Britain 1940, Home Defence
1940-'44

608 Squadron
(North Riding)
Omnibus ungulis (With all talons)
A/c: Mk I Feb '41 to Aug '41
Mk IV Mar '41 to Sep '41
Code: UL Sep '39 to '41
Honours: Baltic 1941-'42

614 Squadron
(County of Glamorgan)
Codaf I geislo (I rise to search)
A/c: Mk IV Jul '41 to Aug '42
Mk V Aug '42 to Jan '44
Code: LJ 1940 to Aug '42

RAF Second Line Units
9, 10, 11, 12 and 13 Group (Gp)
Anti-Aircraft Co-Operation Flight
(Flt);
1, 6, 7, 8 and 22 Anti-Aircraft Co-
Operation Unit;

Aeroplane and Armament
Experimental Est.;
1 Air Armament School;
Air Command SE Asia
Communications (Coms)
Squadron;
Aircraft Delivery Unit;
Air Fighting Development Unit;
Airborne Forces Experimental
Est.;
Advanced Flying Training Unit
(India);
Aircraft Gun Mounting Est.;
1 Air Gunnery School (AGS);
1 (Indian) AS;
Airborne Interception-Air to
Surface Vessel School;
Air Service Training;
1, 3, 5 and 9 Air Observer
School;
Air Sea Rescue (ASR) Flt;
ASR Flt ME (Middle East);
Air Transport Auxiliary;
British Airways Repair Unit;

A line of Blenheim Mk Is of the ATA (Air Transport Auxiliary) School at White Waltham in the spring of 1942. (via Martyn Chorlton)

6, 7, 8 and 1508 Beam Approach Training Flt;
Bombing Development Unit;
5, 7, 9 and 10 Bombing and Gunnery School;
Blenheim Conversion Flt;
3, 17 and 18 Blenheim Delivery Flt;
1 Coast Artillery Co-Operation Flight/Unit;
1 Calibration Flt;
Calibration Flt Blida;
Camouflage Flt;
1 and 2 Camouflage Unit;
3 CDF IAFVR;
1653, East Africa, 13 Gp, 81 Gp, 201 Gp, Hal Far, Hendon, India, Iraq and Khartoum Coms Flt;
Central Flying School;
Central Gunnery School (CGS);
1672 Conversion Unit;
ECFS;
ESW;
2 FF;
Free French Flt;

FIU;
404, 405, 1300, 1301, 1302, 1303, 1401, 1402, 1403, 1404, 1405, 1416, 1434, 1438, 1442, 1438, 1442, 1483, 1508, 1572, 1573, 1578, 1579, 1580, 1581, 1582 and 1653 Flt;
3 Flt Indian Air Force;
35 Flt SAAF;
1482 (Target Towing) Flt;
Sudan Flt;
Y Flt;
Z Flt;
2 and 4 Ferry Pool and Unit;
1, 2, 3, 4, 6 and 7 Ferry Pilots Pool/Unit;
Free French Desert Patrol Flt;
301, 305, 307 and 311 Ferry Training Unit;
9 Ferry Unit;
6 and 9 Flying Training School (FTS);
12 Gp Pool;
2 Gp Training Flt;
2 Gp Target Towing Flt;
India Coms Squadron;

1 and 2 ME Check and Conversion Unit;
1 ME Training School;
3, 4 and 6 ME Training School;
ME Coms Flt;
1655 Mosquito Training Unit;
5, 6, 9, 10, 15, 19, 20, 23, 24, 27, 32, 33, 36, 103, 108, 114, 133, 136, 162, 166, 226, 308, 315, 319 and 326 Maintenance Unit (MU);
North African Practice Flt;
1 Overseas Aircraft Delivery Flt;
1 and 9 Observers Aircraft Delivery Unit;
1, 2, 3, 5, 6, 12, 13, 15, 17, 18, 42, 51, 52, 54, 55, 56, 60, 63, 70, 71, 72, 73, 75, 79, 132 and 152 OTU;
9 and 12 Pilots Advanced Flying Unit;
Photographic Development Unit;
Pilots Reserve and Reinforcement Pool (ME);
Photographic Recce Unit (PRU);
1 PRU;
RAF (ME) CGS;

Mk IF L1132 of 92 Squadron, pictured not long after the unit was reformed at Tangmere in October 1939. (via Martyn Chorlton)

Royal Aircraft Est.;
RAF College;
431 Recce Flt (Malta);
3 Refresher Flying Unit;
2, 3, 4, 5, 6 and 8 Radio MU;
RAF Film Unit;
2 and 3 Radio School;
1, 3, 7, 51 and 54 Radio Servicing
Unit/Section;
2 School of Army Co-Operation;
Special Duties Flt;
Sea Rescue Flt;
Service Ferry Pilots Pool;
17 Service FTS;
Abbotsinch, Andover, Denham,
Dyce, Heston, Odiham and Wyton
Station Flt;
3 School of General Recce;
6 and 10 School of Technical
Training;
Telecommunications Flying
Unit;
Training Unit and Reserve Pool
(ME);
70, 71, 72, 73, 74, 75, 76, 77, 7, 79,
249 and 298 Wing;
74 Wing Calibration Flt.

Fleet Air Arm (FAA)

748 Squadron
A/c: Mk IV Nov '43 to Mar '44

759 Squadron
A/c: Mk IV Jul '43 to Sep '44

762 Squadron
A/c: Mk IV Mar '44 to 1945

770 Squadron
A/c: Mk I Mar '42 to Jun '42
Mk IV Mar '44 to Jun '45

771 Squadron
A/c: Mk I Apr '41 to Jun '43
Mk IV Apr '44 to May '45

772 Squadron
A/c: Mk IV Mar '44 to Apr '45

775 Squadron
A/c: Mk IV May '45 to
Aug '45

776 Squadron
A/c: Mk I Jan '41 to Aug '41
and Apr '44
Mk IV Jan '44 to Apr '45

780 Squadron
A/c: Mk I Jun '43 to Dec '43

787 Squadron
A/c: Mk I Oct '42 to Feb '44
Mk IV Mar '43 to May '45

788 Squadron
A/c: Mk I 1942

798 Squadron
A/c: Mk IV Oct '43 to Mar '44

FOREIGN AIR FORCES
• Croatian Air Force
Operated eight ex-Yugoslav Mk Is

107 Squadron Mk I L1295 on a training sortie from its Wattisham home before the unit's code '107' has been applied. (via Martyn Chorlton)

• **France (Free French)**

The Free French units were Escadrille Topic, GB Bretagne, GB Lorraine, GB 1/20 Loraine (342 Squadron), GRB1, Group 1/17 Picardie, Metz, Nancy and Nantes. All operated the Blenheim Mk IV and Mk Mk V from 1941 until August 1945.

• **Finnish Air Force**
LLv 41

A/c: Mk I Dec '44 to May '45
    Mk IV Dec '44 to 1948

LLv 42

A/c: Mk I Feb '40 to Mk IV

LLv 44

A/c: Mk I Jul '37 to Mk IV

LLv 45

    Mk I, Mk IV

LLv 46

A/c: Mk I Jul '37 to
    Mk IV Feb '40

LLv 48

A/c: Mk IV Oct '44 to May '45

Te-LeR4

A/c: Mk I

1 Lsto

A/c: Mk IV to 1958

• **Hellenic Air Force**
13 (Hellenic) Squadron

A/c: Mk IV Oct '42 to Sep '43
    Mk V Oct '42 to Sep '43

• **Hungarian Air Force**

A/c: Mk I Apr '41 to 1945

• **Portuguese Air Force**
Aviaco Naval (Naval Air Arm)

A/c: Mk IVF and Mk V '43
    to '48

• **Aeronautica Militar (Army Air Force)**

A/c: Mk IV and Mk V
    43 to '48

• **Romanian Air Force**

Fifty-two Blenheims were supplied to the Romanian Air Force in a vain attempt to disrupt the Axis alliances but they all ending up fighting alongside Germany against the Soviet Union from July 1941 until late 1944.

• **Royal Australian Air Force (RAAF)**
454 RAAF Squadron

A/c: Mk V Nov '42 to Jan '43

459 RAAF Squadron

A/c :   V Feb '42 to Mar '42

• **Royal Canadian Air Force (RCAF)**

(All RCAF aircraft are Bolingbrokes)

601 (County of London) Squadron's Mk IFs at a snowy Tangmere in February 1940. (via Martyn Chorlton)

8 (RCAF) Squadron

A/c: Mk I and IV Dec '40 to Aug '43
Code: YO '39 to '42
GA '42 to Aug '43

13 (RCAF) Squadron

A/c: Mk IV Oct '41 to Jun '42
Code: AN '39 to '42
MK '42 to Jun '42

115 (RCAF) Squadron

A/c: Mk I and Mk IV Aug '41 to Aug '43
Code: BK '39 to '42
MK '42 to Aug '43

119 (RCAF) Squadron

A/c: Mk I and Mk IV Jul '40 to Jun '42
Code: DM '39 to '42
GR '42 to Jun '42

121 (RCAF) Squadron

A/c: Mk IV Aug '42 to May '44

Code: EN May '42 to Oct '42

122 (RCAF) Squadron

A/c: Mk IV Aug '42 to Sep '45
Code: AG Aug '42 to Sep '45

147 (RCAF) Squadron

A/c: Mk I and Mk IV Jul '42 to Mar '44
Code: SZ Jul '42 to Sep '45

163 (RCAF) Squadron

A/c: Mk IV Mar '43 to Mar '44

242 (RCAF) Squadron

Toujours prêt (Always ready)
A/c: Mk IF Dec '39 to Dec '39
Code: FC or LE Dec to Dec '41

404 (Buffalo) RCAF Squadron

(Ready to fight)
A/c: Mk I, Mk IF
Mk IVF Apr '41 to Jan '43
Code: EE Apr '41 to Aug '43

406 (Lynx) RCAF Squadron

(We kill by night)
A/c: Mk IF May '41 to Jun '41
Code: HU
Honours: Defence of Britain 1941-'45

407 (Demon) RCAF Squadron (To hold on high)

A/c: Mk IV Dec '41 to Feb '42
Code: GX Aug '41 to Aug '43

415 (Swordfish) RCAF Squadron

Ad metum (To fear)
A/c: Mk IV Dec '41 to Feb '42
Code: RR Dec '41 to Feb '42

• Royal New Zealand Air Force (RNZAF)

489 (RNZAF) Squadron
A/c: Mk IV Jan '42 to Mar '42
Code: XA Jan '42 to Mar '42

604 (County of Middlesex) Mk I at North Weald in September 1939. (via Martyn Chorlton)

- ## Royal Yugoslav Air Force

JKRV (Jugoslovenska Kraljevsko Ratno Vazduhoplovsto)

1 Bomber Regiment, 61 Grupa

201 Eskadrilas

202 Eskadrilas

1 Bomber Regiment, 62 Grupa

203 Eskadrilas

204 Eskadrilas

8 Bomber Regiment, 11 Grupa

21 Eskadrilas

22 Eskadrilas

8 Bomber Regiment, 68 Grupa

215 Eskadrilas

216 Eskadrilas

8 Bomber Regiment, 69 Grupa

217 Eskadrilas

218 Eskadrilas

Independent Long Range Reconnaissance Air Group

- ## South African Air Force (SAAF)

15 (SAAF) Squadron

A/c: Mk V Jul '42 to Jul '43

16 (SAAF) Squadron

A/c: Mk V Nov '42 to Jun '43

17 (SAAF) Squadron

A/c: Mk V Jan '43 to May '43

- ## Turkish Air Force

The Turkish Air Force first began to receive the Blenheim Mk I from 1936, eventually receiving 63 examples across all three marks.

2 Air Division

A/c: Mk I, Mk IV and Mk V '36 to '48

Mk IVs of 57 Squadron operating out of Wyton not long after returning from France in the summer of 1940. (via Martyn Chorlton)